PRACTICE - ASSESS - DIAGNO

180 Days of
PROBLEM SOLVING
for Third Grade

- ❓ Think
- 🔑 Plan
- 💡 Solve
- 🔍 Explain

$$4 \times 6 = 24$$

Author
Kristin Kemp, M.A.Ed.

SHELL EDUCATION

For information on how this resource meets national and other state standards, see pages 4–7. You may also review this information by visiting our website at www.teachercreatedmaterials.com/administrators/correlations/ and following the on-screen directions.

Publishing Credits

Corinne Burton, M.A.Ed., *Publisher*; Conni Medina, M.A.Ed., *Managing Editor*; Emily R. Smith, M.A.Ed., *Series Developer*; Diana Kenney, M.A.Ed., NBCT, *Content Director*; Paula Makridis, M.A.Ed., *Editor*; Lee Aucoin, *Sr. Graphic Designer*; Kyleena Harper, *Assistant Editor*; Kevin Pham, *Graphic Designer*

Image Credits

All images from iStock and Shutterstock.

Standards

Shell Education

A division of Teacher Created Materials
5301 Oceanus Drive
Huntington Beach, CA 92649-1030

www.tcmpub.com/shell-education
ISBN 978-1-4258-1615-5
©2017 Shell Education Publishing, Inc.
Printed in China 51497

TABLE OF CONTENTS

Introduction 3

How to Use this Book 4

Standards Correlations 12

Daily Practice Pages 13

Answer Key. 193

Practice Page Rubric 209

Practice Page Item Analysis. 210

Student Item Analysis. 214

Problem-Solving Framework. 215

Problem-Solving Strategies 216

Digital Resources. 217

INTRODUCTION

The Need for Practice

To be successful in today's mathematics classrooms, students must deeply understand both concepts and procedures so that they can discuss and demonstrate their understanding during the problem-solving process. Demonstrating understanding is a process that must be continually practiced for students to be successful. Practice is especially important to help students apply their concrete, conceptual understanding during each step of the problem-solving process.

Understanding Assessment

In addition to providing opportunities for frequent practice, teachers must be able to assess students' problem-solving skills. This is important so that teachers can adequately address students' misconceptions, build on their current understandings, and challenge them appropriately. Assessment is a long-term process that involves careful analysis of student responses from discussions, projects, practice pages, or tests. When analyzing the data, it is important for teachers to reflect on how their teaching practices may have influenced students' responses and to identify those areas where additional instruction may be required. In short, the data gathered from assessments should be used to inform instruction: slow down, speed up, or reteach. This type of assessment is called *formative assessment*.

HOW TO USE THIS BOOK

180 Days of Problem Solving offers teachers and parents problem-solving activities for each day of the school year. Students will build their problem-solving skills as they develop a deeper understanding of mathematical concepts and apply these concepts to real-life situations. This series will also help students improve their critical-thinking and reasoning skills, use visual models when solving problems, approach problems in multiple ways, and solve multi-step, non-routine word problems.

Easy-to-Use and Standards-Based

These daily activities reinforce grade-level skills across a variety of mathematical concepts. Each day provides a full practice page, making the activities easy to prepare and implement as part of a classroom routine, at the beginning of each mathematics lesson as a warm-up or Problem of the Day, or as homework. Students can work on the practice pages independently or in cooperative groups. The practice pages can also be utilized as diagnostic tools, formative assessments, or summative assessments, which can direct differentiated small-group instruction during Mathematics Workshop.

Domains and Practice Standards

The chart below indicates the mathematics domains addressed and practice standards applied throughout this book. The subsequent chart shows the breakdown of which mathematics standard is covered in each week.

Note: Students may not have a deep understanding of some topics in this book. Remember to assess students based on their problem-solving skills and not exclusively on their content knowledge.

Grade-Level Domains	Standards of Mathematical Practice
1. Operations and Algebraic Thinking 2. Number and Operations in Base Ten 3. Number and Operations—Fractions 4. Measurement and Data 5. Geometry	1. Make sense of problems and persevere in solving them. 2. Reason abstractly and quantitatively. 3. Construct viable arguments and critique the reasoning of others. 4. Model with mathematics. 5. Use appropriate tools strategically. 6. Attend to precision. 7. Look for and make use of structure. 8. Look for and express regularity in repeated reasoning.

HOW TO USE THIS BOOK *(cont.)*

College-and-Career Readiness Standards

Below is a list of mathematical standards that are addressed throughout this book. Each week students solve problems related to the same mathematical topic.

Week	Standard
1	Use place value understanding to round whole numbers to the nearest 10 or 100.
2	Identify arithmetic patterns (including patterns in the addition table), and explain them using properties of operations.
3	Fluently add within 1,000 using strategies and algorithms based on place value, properties of operations, and/or the relationship between addition and subtraction. Solve one-step addition word problems.
4	Fluently subtract within 1,000 using strategies and algorithms based on place value, properties of operations, and/or the relationship between addition and subtraction. Solve one-step subtraction word problems.
5	Solve two-step word problems using addition and subtraction. Represent these problems using equations with a letter standing for the unknown quantity. Assess the reasonableness of answers using mental computation and estimation strategies including rounding.
6	Identify arithmetic patterns (including patterns in the multiplication table), and explain them using properties of operations.
7	Interpret products of whole numbers (e.g., interpret 5×7 as the total number of objects in 5 groups of 7 objects each).
8	Fluently multiply within 100. By the end of grade 3, know from memory all products of two one-digit numbers.
9	Multiply one-digit whole numbers by multiples of 10 in the range of 10–90 (e.g., 9×80, 5×60) using strategies based on place value and properties of operations.
10	Interpret whole-number quotients of whole numbers (e.g., interpret $56 \div 8$ as the number of objects in each share when 56 objects are partitioned equally into 8 shares), or as a number of shares when 56 objects are partitioned into equal shares of 8 objects each.
11	Determine the unknown whole number in a multiplication or division equation relating three whole numbers.
12	Apply properties of operations as strategies to multiply and divide.
13	Understand division as an unknown-factor problem.

HOW TO USE THIS BOOK *(cont.)*

14	Fluently divide within 100, using strategies such as the relationship between multiplication and division (e.g., knowing that $8 \times 5 = 40$, one knows $40 \div 5 = 8$) or properties of operations.
15	Use multiplication and division within 100 to solve word problems in situations involving equal groups, arrays, and measurement quantities (e.g., by using drawings and equations with a symbol for the unknown number to represent the problem).
16	Solve two-step word problems using all four operations. Represent these problems using equations with a letter standing for the unknown quantity. Assess the reasonableness of answers using mental computation and estimation strategies including rounding.
17	Understand a fraction $\frac{1}{b}$ as the quantity formed by 1 part when a whole is partitioned into b equal parts; understand a fraction $\frac{a}{b}$ as the quantity formed by a parts of size $\frac{1}{b}$.
18	Represent a fraction $\frac{1}{b}$ on a number line diagram by defining the interval from 0 to 1 as the whole and partitioning it into b equal parts. Recognize that each part has size $\frac{1}{b}$ and that the endpoint of the part based at 0 locates the number $\frac{1}{b}$ on the number line.
19	Represent a fraction $\frac{a}{b}$ on a number line diagram by marking off a lengths $\frac{1}{b}$ from 0. Recognize that the resulting interval has size $\frac{a}{b}$ and that its endpoint locates the number $\frac{a}{b}$ on the number line.
20	Understand two fractions as equivalent (equal) if they are the same size, or the same point on a number line.
21	Recognize and generate simple equivalent fractions (e.g., $\frac{1}{2} = \frac{2}{4}$, $\frac{4}{6} = \frac{2}{3}$). Explain why the fractions are equivalent (e.g., by using a visual fraction model).
22	Express whole numbers as fractions, and recognize fractions that are equivalent to whole numbers.
23	Compare two fractions with the same numerator or the same denominator by reasoning about their size. Recognize that comparisons are valid only when the two fractions refer to the same whole. Record the results of comparisons with the symbols >, =, or <, and justify the conclusions (e.g., by using a visual fraction model).
24	Tell and write time to the nearest minute and measure time intervals in minutes.
25	Solve word problems involving addition and subtraction of time intervals in minutes (e.g., by representing the problem on a number line diagram).
26	Measure and estimate liquid volumes and masses of objects using standard units of grams (g), kilograms (kg), and liters (l).

HOW TO USE THIS BOOK *(cont.)*

27	Add, subtract, multiply, or divide to solve one-step word problems involving masses or volumes that are given in the same units, e.g., by using drawings (such as a beaker with a measurement scale) to represent the problem.
28	Draw a scaled picture graph to represent a data set with several categories. Solve one- and two-step "how many more" and "how many less" problems using information presented in scaled bar graphs.
29	Draw a scaled bar graph to represent a data set with several categories. Solve one- and two-step "how many more" and "how many less" problems using information presented in scaled bar graphs.
30	Generate measurement data by measuring lengths using rulers marked with halves and fourths of an inch. Show the data by making a line plot, where the horizontal scale is marked off in appropriate units—whole numbers, halves, or quarters.
31	A plane figure that can be covered without gaps or overlaps by *n* unit squares is said to have an area of *n* square units.
32	Measure areas by counting unit squares (square cm, square m, square in., square ft., and improvised units).
33	Multiply side lengths to find areas of rectangles with whole-number side lengths in the context of solving real world and mathematical problems, and represent whole-number products as rectangular areas in mathematical reasoning.
34	Solve real world and mathematical problems involving perimeters of polygons, including finding the perimeter given the side lengths, finding an unknown side length, and exhibiting rectangles with the same perimeter and different areas or with the same area and different perimeters.
35	Understand that shapes in different categories may share attributes and that the shared attributes can define a larger category. Recognize rhombuses, rectangles, and squares as examples of quadrilaterals, and draw examples of quadrilaterals that do not belong to any of these subcategories.
36	Partition shapes into parts with equal areas. Express the area of each part as a unit fraction of the whole.

HOW TO USE THIS BOOK *(cont.)*

Using the Practice Pages

The activity pages provide practice and assessment opportunities for each day of the school year. Students foc us on one grade-level skill each week. The five-day plan requires students to think about the problem-solving process, use visual models, choose multiple strategies, and solve multi-step, non-routine word problems. For this grade level, teachers may complete the pages together as a class, or students may work in cooperative groups. Teachers may prepare packets of weekly practice pages for the classroom or for homework.

Day 1–Think About It!

For the first day of each week, the focus is on thinking about the problem-solving process. Students might draw pictures or answer questions about a problem. The goal is to understand the process of solving a problem more so than finding the solution.

Day 2–Solve It!

On the second day of each week, students solve one to two routine problems based on the thinking process from Day 1. Students think about the information given in the problem, decide on a plan, solve the problem, and look back and explain their work.

Day 3–Visualize It!

On day three, a visual representation (e.g., number line, table, diagram, fraction model) is shown as a strategy for solving a problem. Students use this visual model to solve a similar problem.

Day 4–Solve It Two Ways!

On the fourth day, students solve the same problem two ways by applying the strategies they have learned. Students may also be asked to analyze how others solved a problem and explain which way is correct or state the error or misconception.

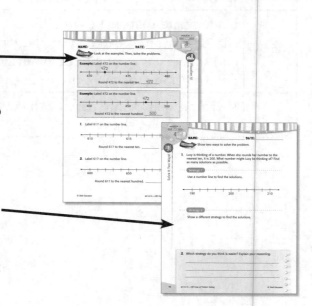

HOW TO USE THIS BOOK *(cont.)*

 Day 5–Challenge Yourself!
On day five, students are presented with a multi-step, non-routine problem. Students analyze a problem, think about different strategies, develop a plan, and explain how they solved the problem.

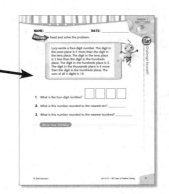

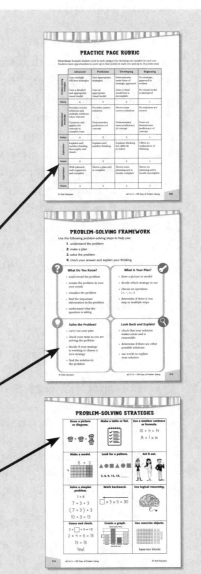

Using the Resources

The following resources will be helpful to students as they complete the activity pages. Print copies of these resources and provide them to students to keep at their desks. These resources are available as Adobe® PDFs online. A complete list of the available documents is provided on page 217. To access the digital resources, go to this website: **http://www.tcmpub.com/download-files**. Enter this code: 01948402. Follow the on-screen directions.

Practice Page Rubric can be found on page 209 and in the Digital Resources (rubric.pdf). The rubric can be used to assess students' mathematical understanding of the weekly concept and steps in the problem-solving process. The rubric should be shared with students so they know what is expected of them.

Problem-Solving Framework can be found on page 215 and in the Digital Resources (framework.pdf). Students can reference each step of the problem-solving process as they complete the practice pages during the week.

Problem-Solving Strategies can be found on page 216 and in the Digital Resources (strategies.pdf). Students may want to reference this page when choosing strategies as they solve problems throughout the week.

HOW TO USE THIS BOOK *(cont.)*

Diagnostic Assessment

Teachers can use the practice pages as diagnostic assessments. The data analysis tools included with the book enable teachers or parents to quickly score students' work and monitor their progress. Teachers and parents can quickly see which steps in the problem-solving process students need to target further to develop proficiency.

After students complete a week of practice pages, each page can be graded using the answer key (pages 193–208). Then, the *Practice Page Rubric* (page 209; rubric.pdf) can be used to score each practice page. The *Practice Page Item Analysis* (pages 210–213; itemanalysis.pdf) can be completed. The *Practice Page Item Analysis* can be used to record students' Day 5 practice page score, while the *Student Item Analysis* (page 214; studentitem.pdf) can be used to record a student's daily practice page score. These charts are also provided in the Digital Resources as PDFs, Microsoft Word® files (itemanalysis.docx; studentitem.docx), and Microsoft Excel® files (itemanalysis.xlsx; studentitem.xlsx). Teachers can input data into the electronic files directly on the computer, or they can print the pages and analyze students' work using paper and pencil.

To Complete the Practice Page Item Analysis

- Write or type students' names in the far-left column. Depending on the number of students, more than one copy of the form may be needed, or you may need to add rows.

- The specific week is indicated across the top of each chart.

- Record rubric scores for the Day 5 practice page in the appropriate column.

- Add the scores for each student. Place that sum in the far-right column. Use these scores as benchmarks to determine how each student is performing after a nine-week period. This allows for four benchmarks during the year that can be used to gather formative diagnostic data.

HOW TO USE THIS BOOK *(cont.)*

To Complete the Student Item Analysis

- Write or type the student's name in the top row. This form tracks the ongoing process of each student, so one copy per student is necessary.

- The specific day is indicated across the top of each chart.

- Record the student's rubric score for each practice page in the appropriate column.

- Add the scores for the student. Place that sum in the far-right column. Use these scores as benchmarks to determine how the student is performing each week. These benchmarks can be used to gather formative diagnostic data.

Using the Results to Differentiate Instruction

Once results are gathered and analyzed, teachers can use the results to inform the way they differentiate instruction. The data can help determine which mathematical concepts and steps in the problem-solving process are the most difficult for students and which students need additional instructional support and continued practice.

Whole-Class Support

The results of the diagnostic analysis may show that the entire class is struggling with a particular mathematical concept or problem-solving step. If these concepts or problem-solving steps have been taught in the past, this indicates that further instruction or reteaching is necessary. If these concepts or steps have not been taught in the past, this data may indicate that students do not have a working knowledge of the concepts or steps. Thus, careful planning for the length of the unit(s) or lesson(s) must be considered, and additional front-loading may be required.

Small-Group or Individual Support

The results of the diagnostic analysis may show that an individual student or small group of students is struggling with a particular mathematical concept or problem-solving step. If these concepts or steps have been taught in the past, this indicates that further instruction or reteaching is necessary. These students can be pulled to a small group for further instruction on the concept(s) or step(s), while other students work independently. Students may also benefit from extra practice using games or computer-based resources. Teachers can also use the results to help identify individual students or groups of proficient students who are ready for enrichment or above-grade-level instruction. These groups may benefit from independent learning contracts or more challenging activities.

Digital Resources

The Digital Resources contain diagnostic pages and additional resources, such as the *Problem-Solving Framework* and *Problem-Solving Strategies* pages, for students. The list of resources in the Digital Resources can be found on page 217.

STANDARDS CORRELATIONS

Shell Education is committed to producing educational materials that are research- and standards-based. In this effort, we have correlated all of our products to the academic standards of all 50 states, the District of Columbia, the Department of Defense Dependents Schools, and all Canadian provinces.

How to Find Standards Correlations

To print a customized correlation report of this product for your state, visit our website at **http://www.tcmpub.com/shell-education**. If you require assistance in printing correlation reports, please contact our Customer Service Department at 1-877-777-3450.

Purpose and Intent of Standards

The Every Student Succeeds Act (ESSA) mandates that all states adopt challenging academic standards that help students meet the goal of college and career readiness. While many states already adopted academic standards prior to ESSA, the act continues to hold states accountable for detailed and comprehensive standards.

Standards are designed to focus instruction and guide adoption of curricula. Standards are statements that describe the criteria necessary for students to meet specific academic goals. They define the knowledge, skills, and content students should acquire at each level. Standards are also used to develop standardized tests to evaluate students' academic progress.

Teachers are required to demonstrate how their lessons meet state standards. State standards are used in the development of all of our products, so educators can be assured they meet the academic requirements of each state.

The activities in this book are aligned to today's national and state-specific college-and-career readiness standards. The chart on page 4 lists the domains and practice standards addressed throughout this book. A more detailed chart on pages 5–7 correlates the specific mathematics content standards to each week.

NAME: _____ DATE: _____

 DIRECTIONS: Think about the problem. Answer the questions.

What is the greatest number you can make with these digits?

 2 7 4 6

1. How can you use what you know about place value to help you solve the problem?

_____

_____

_____

2. Which digit should be written in the ones place value? Explain how you know.

_____

_____

_____

Solve It!

NAME: _____ DATE: _____

DIRECTIONS: Read and solve each problem.

Problem 1: What is the greatest number you can make with these digits?

2   7   4   6

? What Do You Know?

🔑 What Is Your Plan?

💡 Solve the Problem!

🔍 Look Back and Explain!

Problem 2: What is the least number you can make with these digits?

9   3   1   5

? What Do You Know?

🔑 What Is Your Plan?

💡 Solve the Problem!

🔍 Look Back and Explain!

NAME: _____ **DATE:** _____

DIRECTIONS: Look at the examples. Then, solve the problems.

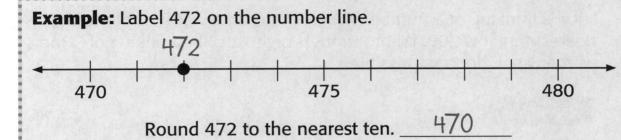

Example: Label 472 on the number line.

472

470   475   480

Round 472 to the nearest ten. __470__

Example: Label 472 on the number line.

472

400   450   500

Round 472 to the nearest hundred. __500__

1. Label 617 on the number line.

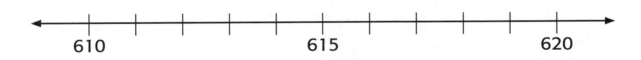

610   615   620

Round 617 to the nearest ten. _____

2. Label 617 on the number line.

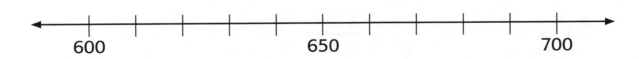

600   650   700

Round 617 to the nearest hundred. _____

Solve It Two Ways!

NAME: _____ DATE: _____

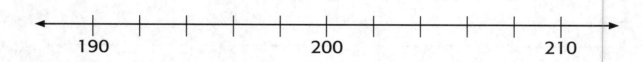

DIRECTIONS: Show two ways to solve the problem.

1. Lucy is thinking of a number. When she rounds her number to the nearest ten, it is 200. What number might Lucy be thinking of? Find as many solutions as possible.

Strategy 1

Use a number line to find the solutions.

```
◄───┼────┼────┼────┼────┼────┼────┼────┼────┼────┼────►
   190                  200                      210
```

Strategy 2

Show a different strategy to find the solutions.

2. Which strategy do you think is easier? Explain your reasoning.

_____

_____

_____

NAME: _____ **DATE:** _____

DIRECTIONS: Read and solve the problem.

> Lucy wrote a four-digit number. The digit in the ones place is 5 more than the digit in the tens place. The digit in the tens place is 2 less than the digit in the hundreds place. The digit in the hundreds place is 3. The digit in the thousands place is 6 more than the digit in the hundreds place. The sum of all 4 digits is 19.

1. What is the four-digit number?

2. What is this number rounded to the nearest ten? _____

3. What is this number rounded to the nearest hundred? _____

Show Your Thinking

Think About It!

NAME: _____ **DATE:** _____

DIRECTIONS: Look at the number line. Answer the questions.

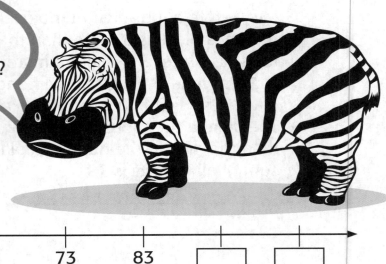

What are the next two numbers in the pattern?

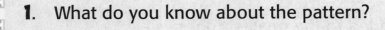

43   53   63   73   83   ☐   ☐

1. What do you know about the pattern?

_____

_____

_____

_____

2. What do you need to find to solve the problem?

_____

_____

_____

_____

NAME: _____ **DATE:** _____

 DIRECTIONS: Read and solve each problem.

Problem 1: What are the next two numbers in the pattern?

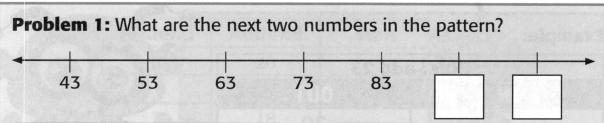

43   53   63   73   83   ☐   ☐

| ? What Do You Know? | ⚷ What Is Your Plan? |
| 💡 Solve the Problem! | 🔍 Look Back and Explain! |

Problem 2: What are the next two numbers in the pattern?

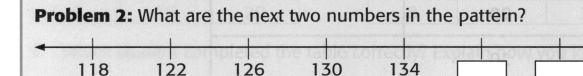

118   122   126   130   134   ☐   ☐

| ? What Do You Know? | ⚷ What Is Your Plan? |
| 💡 Solve the Problem! | 🔍 Look Back and Explain! |

NAME: _____ **DATE:** _____

DIRECTIONS: Read and solve the problem.

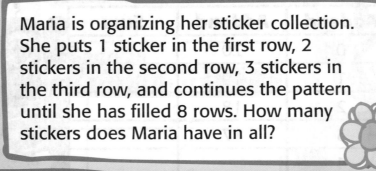

Maria is organizing her sticker collection. She puts 1 sticker in the first row, 2 stickers in the second row, 3 stickers in the third row, and continues the pattern until she has filled 8 rows. How many stickers does Maria have in all?

1. Choose a strategy to show the pattern.

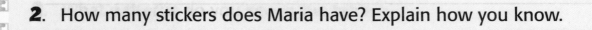

2. How many stickers does Maria have? Explain how you know.

_____

_____

_____

_____

NAME: _____ **DATE:** _____

 **DIRECTIONS:** Think about the problem. Answer the questions.

Mrs. Morales writes a number in expanded form on the board. She asks her students to find the mystery number. What is the number?

$$5,000 + 900 + 30 + 2 = \underline{\hspace{2cm}}$$

1. How might you solve the problem?

_____

_____

_____

2. How does understanding place value help you solve the problem?

_____

_____

_____

_____

Solve It!

NAME: _____ DATE: _____

DIRECTIONS: Read and solve each problem.

Problem 1: Mrs. Morales writes a number in expanded form on the board. She asks her students to find the mystery number. What is the number?

$$5,000 + 900 + 30 + 2 = \underline{\hspace{1.5cm}}$$

? What Do You Know?

🔑 What Is Your Plan?

💡 Solve the Problem!

🔍 Look Back and Explain!

Problem 2: Mrs. Morales writes another problem on the board. What is the mystery number?

$$2,000 + 700 + 10 + 1 = \underline{\hspace{1.5cm}}$$

? What Do You Know?

🔑 What Is Your Plan?

💡 Solve the Problem!

🔍 Look Back and Explain!

NAME: _____ **DATE:** _____

 DIRECTIONS: Look at the example. Then, solve the problem using the number line.

Example: 153 + 129 = ☐

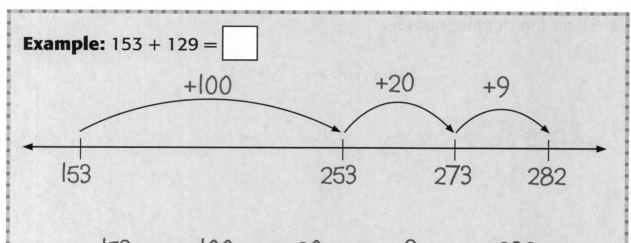

+100   +20   +9

153   253   273   282

__153__ + __100__ + __20__ + __9__ = __282__

153 + 129 = __282__

235 + 164 = ☐

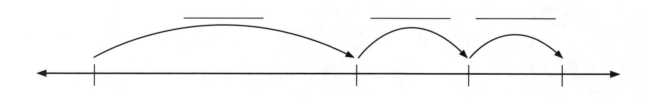

_____ + _____ + _____ + _____ = _____

235 + 164 = _____

Solve It Two Ways!

NAME: _____ **DATE:** _____

DIRECTIONS: Show two ways to solve the problem.

1. Find the missing number.

$$355 + 150 = \boxed{} + 275$$

. . . . Strategy 1 . . . .

. . . . Strategy 2 . . . .

2. Which strategy do you think is better? Explain your reasoning.

_____

_____

_____

NAME: _____ **DATE:** _____

DIRECTIONS: Read and solve the problem.

Students at Pine Lake Elementary School are having a bake sale to raise money for a local animal shelter. On Monday, they sold 167 cookies and 233 cupcakes. On Tuesday, they sold 329 cookies and 137 cupcakes. How many baked items did they sell in all?

1. Choose a strategy to solve the problem. Show your work.

2. On which day did the students sell more baked items? How do you know?

_____

_____

_____

_____

Think About It!

NAME: _____ **DATE:** _____

DIRECTIONS: Think about the problem. Then, answer the questions.

Do you see a pattern?

9 – 5

90 – 50

900 – 500

9,000 – 5,000

1. What pattern do you see?

_____

_____

_____

_____

2. Can you find 900 – 50 using this pattern? Explain your reasoning.

_____

_____

_____

_____

NAME: _____ **DATE:** _____

 **DIRECTIONS:** Read and solve each problem.

Problem 1: 9 − 5 = _____   900 − 500 = _____

90 − 50 = _____   9,000 − 5,000 = _____

? What Do You Know?

🔑 What Is Your Plan?

💡 Solve the Problem!

🔍 Look Back and Explain!

Problem 1: 15 − 8 = _____   1,500 − 800 = _____

_____ − 80 = 70   15,000 − _____ = 7,000

? What Do You Know?

🔑 What Is Your Plan?

💡 Solve the Problem!

🔍 Look Back and Explain!

NAME: _____ **DATE:** _____

DIRECTIONS: Look at the example. Then, solve the problem using the number line.

Visualize It!

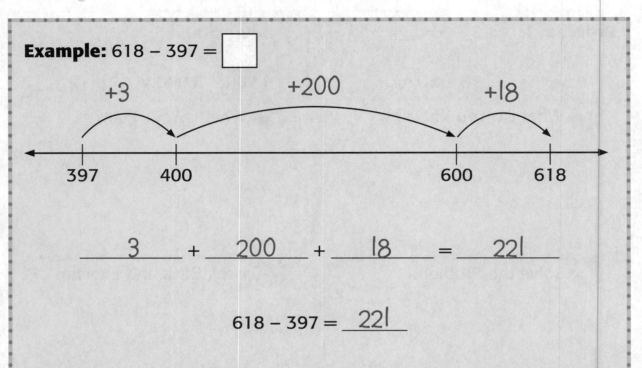

Example: $618 - 397 =$ ☐

+3   +200   +18

397   400   600   618

___3___ + ___200___ + ___18___ = ___221___

$618 - 397 =$ ___221___

$562 - 279 =$ ☐

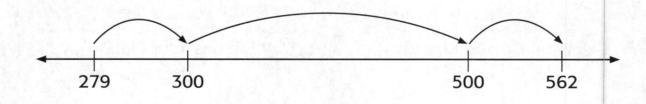

279   300   500   562

_____ + _____ + _____ = _____

$562 - 279 =$ _____

NAME: _____ **DATE:** _____

DIRECTIONS: Show two ways to solve the problem.

1. On Monday, a flower shop had 740 roses. By Saturday, there were 329 roses left. How many roses did the flower shop sell?

Strategy 1

Strategy 2

2. Which strategy do you like better? Explain your reasoning.

_____

_____

_____

NAME: _____ **DATE:** _____

DIRECTIONS: Read and solve the problem.

Aiden is reading a book with 305 pages. During school, he reads 26 pages. Before bed, he reads 57 pages. How many pages of the book does he have left to read?

1. Choose a strategy to solve the problem. Show your work.

2. How can you check your answer? Explain your thinking.

_____

_____

_____

_____

NAME: _____ DATE: _____

DIRECTIONS: Think about the problem. Answer the questions.

Shawn has 65 crayons. He gives some to his sister. He has 38 crayons left.

1. What information is given?

   _____

   _____

   _____

   _____

2. Write a question that can be answered from this information.

   _____

   _____

   _____

Solve It!

NAME: _____ **DATE:** _____

DIRECTIONS: Read and solve each problem.

Problem 1: Shawn has 65 crayons. He gives some to his sister. He has 38 crayons left. How many crayons did Shawn give to his sister?

? What Do You Know?

🔑 What Is Your Plan?

💡 Solve the Problem!

🔍 Look Back and Explain!

Problem 2: Kevin has many comic books. He gave away 14 old books. He has 62 comic books left. How many books did he start with?

? What Do You Know?

🔑 What Is Your Plan?

💡 Solve the Problem!

🔍 Look Back and Explain!

NAME: _____ **DATE:** _____

 **DIRECTIONS:** Look at the example. Then, solve the problem by completing the table.

Example: Marcella's Pizzeria makes a lot of pizzas during the week. Estimate to find about how many pizzas they made last week. Round your answers to the nearest hundred.

Type of pizza	Actual number of pizzas	Estimated number of pizzas
pepperoni	567	600
cheese	460	500
sausage	341	300
Total		1,400

Marcella's Pizzeria also makes other types of food. Estimate to find about how many other food items they made last week. Round your answers to the nearest hundred.

Type of food	Actual number of food items	Estimated number of food items
salad	636	
sandwiches	380	
breadsticks	229	
Total		

NAME: _____ **DATE:** _____

Solve It Two Ways!

DIRECTIONS: Show two ways to solve the problem.

1. A bus picked up 32 people at the first stop. At the second stop, 12 people got off. At the next stop, 6 more people got off, but 10 got on. How many people are on the bus now?

Strategy 1

Strategy 2

2. Which strategy do you think is better? Explain your reasoning.

_____

_____

_____

NAME: _____ DATE: _____

DIRECTIONS: Read and solve the problem.

Dr. Callahan is a school principal. She wants to write a positive note to every student attending her school. There are 360 students in her school. She will write 60 notes a week. After 4 weeks, how many notes will she have left to write?

1. How many notes will Dr. Callahan write in 4 weeks? Explain how you know.

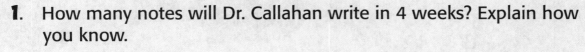

_____

_____

2. What is the solution? Use words, numbers, or pictures to show your work.

Think About It!

NAME: _____ **DATE:** _____

DIRECTIONS: Look at the multiplication table. Then, answer the questions.

×	1	2	3	4
1	1	2	?	4
2	?	4	6	?
3	3	6	?	12
4	4	8	12	?

1. How can you use this chart to find a product?

_____

_____

_____

2. Describe one pattern you see in the multiplication table.

_____

_____

_____

_____

NAME: _____ **DATE:** _____

 **DIRECTIONS:** Read and solve each problem.

Problem 1: Find the missing products in the multiplication table.

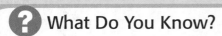 **What Do You Know?**

 **What Is Your Plan?**

×	1	2	3	4
1	1	2		4
2		4	6	
3	3	6		12
4	4	8	12	

Solve the Problem!

Look Back and Explain!

Problem 2: Find the missing products in the multiplication table.

What Do You Know?

×	5	6	7	8
2	10	12		16
3		18		24
4	20		28	
5			35	40

What Is Your Plan?

Solve the Problem!

Look Back and Explain!

NAME: _____ DATE: _____

DIRECTIONS: Look at the example. Then, solve the problem by completing the table.

Example:

Rule: × 3	
In	**Out**
1	3
2	6
3	9
4	12

$1 \times 3 = 3$
$2 \times 3 = 6$
$3 \times 3 = 9$
$4 \times 3 = 12$

Do you see the pattern?

1.

Rule: × 5	
In	**Out**
1	
2	
3	
4	

2. What patterns do you see in the table?

_____

_____

_____

_____

 #51615—180 Days of Problem Solving

NAME: _____ **DATE:** _____

DIRECTIONS: Show two ways to solve the problem.

1. Jasmine is buying cards to invite friends to her birthday party. She needs 40 cards total. She buys 4 packs of cards. Each pack has 8 cards inside. Does Jasmine have enough cards?

Strategy 1 ·

Strategy 2 ·

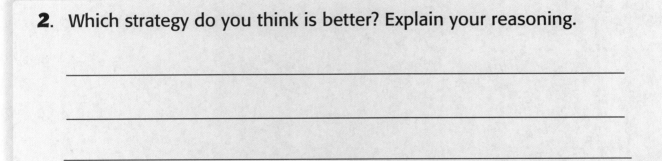

2. Which strategy do you think is better? Explain your reasoning.

_____

_____

_____

NAME: _____ DATE: _____

DIRECTIONS: Read and solve the problem.

Hannah is helping her grandmother plant flowers in her garden. They want flowers in 6 different sections. Each section will have 3 rows of flowers with 3 flowers in each row. How many flowers will they plant in all?

1. How many flowers are in each section of the garden? How do you know?

_____

_____

_____

2. What is the solution? Use words, numbers, or pictures to show your work.

NAME: _____ **DATE:** _____

DIRECTIONS: Think about the problem. Answer the questions.

Alex is buying bags of apples to bake some pies. He buys 3 bags. There are 4 apples in each bag. How many apples does Alex buy in all?

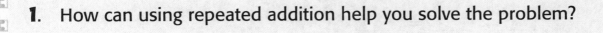

1. How can using repeated addition help you solve the problem?

   _____

   _____

   _____

   _____

2. How can using multiplication help you solve the problem?

   _____

   _____

   _____

   _____

NAME: _____ **DATE:** _____

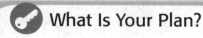 **DIRECTIONS:** Read and solve each problem.

Problem 1: Alex is buying bags of apples to bake some pies. He buys 3 bags. There are 4 apples in each bag. How many apples does Alex buy in all?

? What Do You Know?

🔑 What Is Your Plan?

💡 Solve the Problem!

_____ + _____ + _____ = _____

_____ × _____ = _____

🔍 Look Back and Explain!

Problem 2: Alex also wants to bake some peach pies. He buys 4 bags. There are 5 peaches in each bag. How many peaches does he buy?

? What Do You Know?

🔑 What Is Your Plan?

💡 Solve the Problem!

_____ + _____ + _____ = _____

_____ × _____ = _____

🔍 Look Back and Explain!

NAME: _____ **DATE:** _____

 **DIRECTIONS:** Look at the example. Then, complete the problem.

Example: Make a rectangular array of squares to show 4 × 6.

$4 \times 6 = \underline{24}$

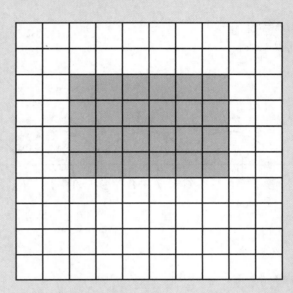

Make a rectangular array of squares to show 7 × 3.

$7 \times 3 = \underline{\hspace{1cm}}$

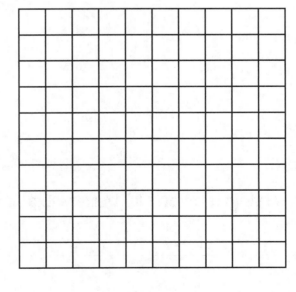

NAME: _____ **DATE:** _____

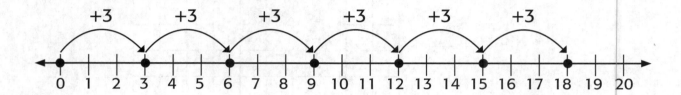

DIRECTIONS: Look at the first strategy used to solve the problem. Then, solve it a different way.

1. What is the product of 6 × 3?

····· Strategy 1 ··

```
    +3      +3      +3      +3      +3      +3

  0  1  2  3  4  5  6  7  8  9 10 11 12 13 14 15 16 17 18 19 20
```

····· Strategy 2 ··

2. Which strategy do you like better? Explain your reasoning.

_____

_____

_____

NAME: _____ **DATE:** _____

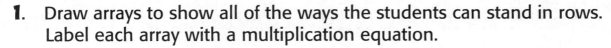

DIRECTIONS: Read and solve the problem.

It is picture day in Mrs. Wong's class. There are 24 students in the class. The photographer wants the students to stand in equal rows. Each row must have more than 1 student. How many ways can the students stand in rows?

1. Draw arrays to show all of the ways the students can stand in rows. Label each array with a multiplication equation.

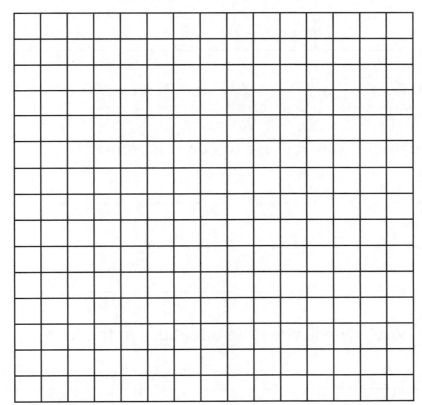

2. How many arrays did you draw? What patterns do you see?

_____

_____

Think About It!

NAME: _____ **DATE:** _____

DIRECTIONS: Think about the problem. Answer the questions.

Write the equations in the correct section of the table.

$4 \times 5 = \boxed{}$ $3 \times 6 = \boxed{}$ $2 \times 10 = \boxed{}$ $5 \times 5 = \boxed{}$

Product < 20	Product = 20	Product > 20

1. What strategies can you use to find the products?

   _____

   _____

   _____

2. Explain how you will write the equations in the table.

   _____

   _____

   _____

   _____

NAME: _____ **DATE:** _____

 **DIRECTIONS:** Read and solve each problem.

Solve It!

Problem 1: Write the equations in the correct section of the table.

$4 \times 5 =$ _____ $3 \times 6 =$ _____ $2 \times 10 =$ _____ $5 \times 5 =$ _____

Product < 20	Product = 20	Product > 20

 What Do You Know?

What Is Your Plan?

 Solve the Problem!

Look Back and Explain!

Problem 2: Write the equations in the correct section of the table.

$6 \times 7 =$ _____ $9 \times 4 =$ _____ $8 \times 5 =$ _____ $4 \times 10 =$ _____

Product < 40	Product = 40	Product > 40

 What Do You Know?

What Is Your Plan?

 Solve the Problem!

 Look Back and Explain!

Visualize It!

NAME: _____ DATE: _____

DIRECTIONS: Look at the example. Then, solve the problem.

Example: Break apart the first factor into two addends. Use them as factors to find the product.

$7 \times 8 = \boxed{}$

$5 + \underline{2}$

$\underline{5} \times \underline{8} = \underline{40}$

$\underline{2} \times \underline{8} = \underline{16}$

$\underline{40} + \underline{16} = \underline{56}$

1. Break apart the first factor into two addends. Use them as factors to find the product.

$8 \times 6 = \boxed{}$

$5 + \underline{}$

$\underline{5} \times \underline{} = \underline{}$

$\underline{} \times \underline{} = \underline{}$

$\underline{} + \underline{} = \underline{}$

2. Break apart the first factor into two addends. Use them as factors to find the product.

$6 \times 9 = \boxed{}$

$3 + \underline{}$

$\underline{3} \times \underline{} = \underline{}$

$\underline{} \times \underline{} = \underline{}$

$\underline{} + \underline{} = \underline{}$

NAME: _____ **DATE:** _____

DIRECTIONS: Show two ways to solve the problem.

1. Antonio is running for class president. He made flyers for his campaign. Eight of his friends will help hand them out. Each friend has 9 flyers. How many flyers will they hand out?

Strategy 1

Strategy 2

2. Which strategy do you prefer? Explain your reasoning.

_____

_____

_____

NAME: _____ **DATE:** _____

DIRECTIONS: Read and solve the problem.

> Use the numbers to write as many multiplication facts as possible with the product 36. Use each number at least once.
>
> 2   4   36   12   6   3   18   1   9

1. List all of the equations.

2. How many equations did you write? _____

3. Do you see a pattern with some of the equations you wrote? Explain your answer.

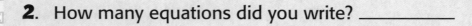

_____

_____

_____

_____

_____

NAME: _____ **DATE:** _____

DIRECTIONS: Look at the problem. Then, answer the questions.

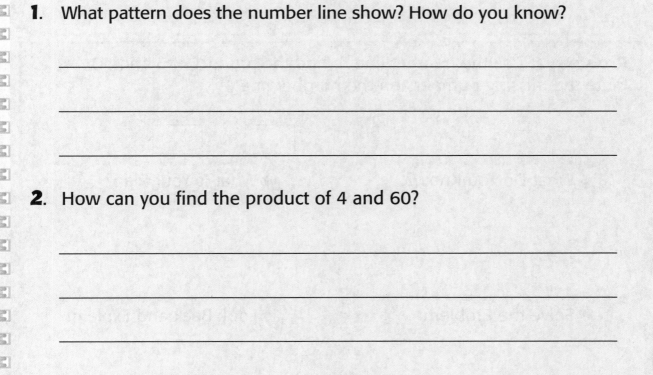

Use the number line to find the product of 4 and 60.

0   60   120   180   [ ]

1. What pattern does the number line show? How do you know?

_____

_____

_____

2. How can you find the product of 4 and 60?

_____

_____

_____

_____

Solve It!

NAME: _____ DATE: _____

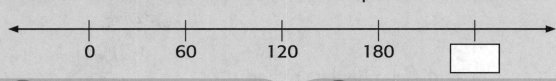

DIRECTIONS: Read and solve each problem.

Problem 1: Use the number line to find the product of 4 and 60.

0   60   120   180   [ ]

What Do You Know?

What Is Your Plan?

Solve the Problem!

Look Back and Explain!

Problem 2: Use the number line to find the product of 3 and 50. Write the missing numbers on the number line.

0   50   [ ]   [ ]

What Do You Know?

What Is Your Plan?

Solve the Problem!

Look Back and Explain!

NAME: _____ **DATE:** _____

 DIRECTIONS: Look at the example. Then, solve the problem.

Example: Draw base-ten blocks to show 7 × 20. Draw a circle around groups of 100.

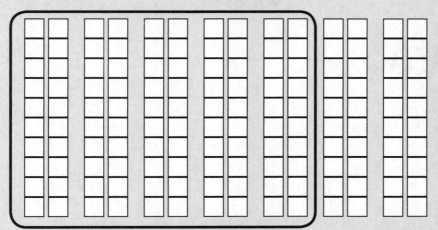

____7____ groups of ____2____ tens = ____14____ tens

7 × 20 = ____140____

Draw base-ten blocks to show 6 × 30. Draw a circle around groups of 100.

_____ groups of _____ tens = _____ tens

6 × 30 = _____

Solve It Two Ways!

NAME: _____ **DATE:** _____

DIRECTIONS: Show two ways to solve the problem.

1.

$$6 \times 70 = \boxed{}$$

Strategy 1 ·

Strategy 2 ·

2. Which strategy do you think is easier? Explain your reasoning.

_____

_____

_____

NAME: _____ **DATE:** _____

DIRECTIONS: Read and solve the problem.

Stacy has 10 boxes of markers. Five of the boxes have 20 markers each. The other 5 boxes have 30 markers each. How many markers does she have in all?

1. Draw a model to show your work.

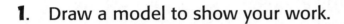

2. What is the solution? Explain how you found your answer.

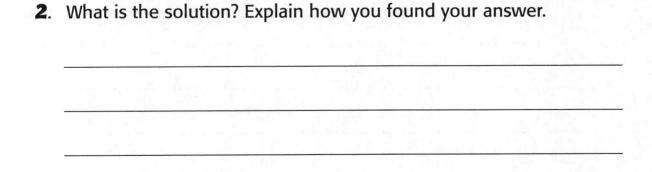

_____

_____

_____

_____

Think About It!

NAME: _____ **DATE:** _____

DIRECTIONS: Think about the problem. Then, answer the questions.

There are 8 goldfish divided into 4 bowls. Each bowl has the same number of fish. How many fish are in each bowl? Write a division equation to show the problem.

1. What information is given to you?

_____

_____

_____

2. How can you solve the problem?

_____

_____

_____

_____

NAME: _____ **DATE:** _____

 **DIRECTIONS:** Read and solve each problem.

Problem 1: There are 8 goldfish divided into 4 bowls. Each bowl has the same number of fish. How many fish are in each bowl? Write a division equation to show the problem.

 What Do You Know?

What Is Your Plan?

 Solve the Problem!

 $\square \div \square = \square$

_____ fish in each bowl

Look Back and Explain!

Problem 2: There are 18 turtles divided into 3 tanks. Each tank has the same number of turtles. How many turtles are in each tank? Write a division equation to show the problem.

 What Do You Know?

 What Is Your Plan?

 Solve the Problem!

 $\square \div \square = \square$

_____ turtles in each tank

 Look Back and Explain!

Visualize It!

NAME: _____ DATE: _____

DIRECTIONS: Look at the example. Then, solve the problem by completing the table.

Example:

Total	Number of equal groups	Number in each group	Division fact
16	4	4	16 ÷ 4 = 4
45	5	9	45 ÷ 5 = 9
36	9	4	36 ÷ 9 = 4
14	7	2	14 ÷ 7 = 2

1.

Total	Number of equal groups	Number in each group	Division fact
56	8		
	10	5	
28	4		
64		8	

2.

Total	Number of equal groups	Number in each group	Division fact
12	2		
20		5	
	6	3	
72		9	

NAME: _____ **DATE:** _____

DIRECTIONS: Show two ways to solve the problem.

1. Jared has 72 baseball cards. He sorts them into 9 piles. Each pile has the same number of cards. How many cards are in each pile?

Strategy 1

Strategy 2

2. Which strategy do you think is easier? Explain your reasoning.

_____

_____

_____

NAME: _____ DATE: _____

DIRECTIONS: Read and solve the problem.

Maddie has 13 sports trophies. She wants to put an equal number of trophies on 3 shelves. How many trophies will go on each shelf? How many trophies will be left over?

1. Draw a picture to solve the problem.

2. How can you change the number of trophies so that there will not be any left over? Explain your reasoning.

_____

_____

_____

NAME: _____ DATE: _____

 DIRECTIONS: Think about the problem. Then, answer the questions.

Jessica has 63 seashells. She divides them into some bags. There are 9 seashells in each bag. How many bags does Jessica use? Find the missing number in the division equation.

$$63 \div \boxed{} = 9$$

1. What information is given?

_____

_____

_____

2. How can you find the missing number in this equation?

_____

_____

_____

_____

NAME: _____ **DATE:** _____

Solve It!

DIRECTIONS: Read and solve the problem.

Problem: Jessica has 63 seashells. She divides them into some bags. There are 9 seashells in each bag. How many bags does Jessica use? Find the missing number in the division equation.

$$63 \div \boxed{} = 9$$

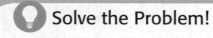 **What Do You Know?**

 **What Is Your Plan?**

Solve the Problem!

Look Back and Explain!

NAME: _____ DATE: _____

DIRECTIONS: Look at the example. Then, solve the problem.

Visualize It!

Example: On Saturday afternoon, 40 cars were parked in the parking lot. There were 8 cars in each row. How many rows of cars were there? Draw an array to solve the problem.

Find the missing number in the division equation.

$$40 \div \underline{\quad 5 \quad} = 8$$

Answer: _____5 rows_____

On Sunday evening, 20 cars were parked in the parking lot. There were 5 cars in each row. How many rows of cars were there?
Draw an array to solve the problem.

Find the missing number in the division equation.

$$20 \div \underline{\quad\quad} = 5$$

Answer: _____

Solve It Two Ways!

NAME: _____ **DATE:** _____

DIRECTIONS: Show two ways to solve the problem.

1. Vinita's dog eats 3 cups of dog food every day. She is going on vacation and leaves the dog sitter 24 cups of food. How many days will Vinita be on vacation?

Strategy 1

Strategy 2

2. Which strategy do you like better? Explain your reasoning.

_____

_____

_____

© Shell Education

NAME: _____ **DATE:** _____

 DIRECTIONS: Read and solve the problem.

James and Matt are having a disagreement over a math problem. James says the only possible answer is 16. Matt says the only possible answer is 4. Who is correct?

$$2 = \boxed{} \div 8$$

1. Draw a picture to show your answer.

2. Who do you agree with? Explain your reasoning.

_____

_____

_____

3. Explain why the other person is wrong.

_____

_____

Think About It!

NAME: _____ **DATE:** _____

DIRECTIONS: Think about the problem. Then, answer the questions.

Find the missing factor in the multiplication equation.

$$9 \times 3 = \boxed{} \times 9$$

1. What do you know about the equation?

_____

_____

_____

2. How can you find the missing factor?

_____

_____

_____

_____

NAME: _____ **DATE:** _____

 DIRECTIONS: Read and solve each problem.

Problem 1: Find the missing factor in the multiplication equation.

$$9 \times 3 = \boxed{} \times 9$$

? What Do You Know?

🔑 What Is Your Plan?

💡 Solve the Problem!

🔍 Look Back and Explain!

Problem 2: Find the missing factor in the multiplication equation.

$$6 \times \boxed{} = 7 \times 6$$

? What Do You Know?

🔑 What Is Your Plan?

💡 Solve the Problem!

🔍 Look Back and Explain!

Visualize It!

NAME: _____ **DATE:** _____

DIRECTIONS: Look at the example. Then, solve the problem.

Example: Use the area model to complete the equations.

$4 \times 7 = 4 \times (5 + 2)$

$4 \times 7 = (4 \times \underline{5}) + (4 \times \underline{2})$

$4 \times 7 = \underline{20} + 8$

$4 \times 7 = \underline{28}$

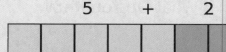

Use the area model to complete the equations.

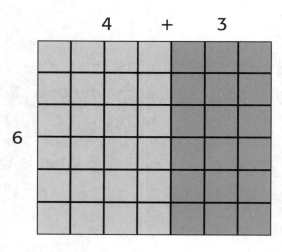

$6 \times 7 = 6 \times (4 + 3)$

$6 \times 7 = (6 \times \underline{\hspace{1cm}}) + (6 \times \underline{\hspace{1cm}})$

$6 \times 7 = \underline{\hspace{1cm}} + 18$

$6 \times 7 = \underline{\hspace{1cm}}$

NAME: _____ **DATE:** _____

DIRECTIONS: Show two ways to solve the problem.

Solve It Two Ways!

1. Leo collects model cars. He keeps his collection of cars on 4 shelves. Each shelf has 5 rows of cars with 3 cars in each row. How many cars does Leo have in all?

Strategy 1 ·

Strategy 2 ·

2. Which strategy do you like better? Explain your reasoning.

_____

_____

_____

Challenge Yourself!

NAME: _____ **DATE:** _____

DIRECTIONS: Read and solve the problem.

Olivia thinks the equation is false. How can you show Olivia that the equation is true?

$$4 \times 3 \times 2 = 8 \times 3$$

1. Draw a picture to show the equation.

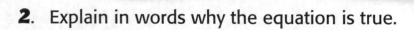

2. Explain in words why the equation is true.

_____

_____

_____

_____

NAME: _____ **DATE:** _____

 DIRECTIONS: Think about the problem. Then, answer the questions.

Write four equations using the numbers in this fact family.

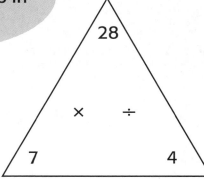

28

×   ÷

7   4

1. How many multiplication equations can you write? _____

2. How many division equations can you write? _____

3. Does the order of the numbers matter? Explain your thinking.

_____

_____

_____

_____

_____

_____

Solve It!

NAME: _____ DATE: _____

DIRECTIONS: Read and solve each problem.

Problem 1: Write four equations using the numbers in this fact family.

28   7   4

? What Do You Know?

What Is Your Plan?

Solve the Problem!

_____ × _____ = _____

_____ × _____ = _____

_____ ÷ _____ = _____

_____ ÷ _____ = _____

Look Back and Explain!

Problem 2: Write four equations using the numbers in this fact family.

54   6   9

? What Do You Know?

What Is Your Plan?

Solve the Problem!

_____ × _____ = _____

_____ × _____ = _____

_____ ÷ _____ = _____

_____ ÷ _____ = _____

Look Back and Explain!

NAME: _____ **DATE:** _____

DIRECTIONS: Look at the example. Then, solve the problem.

Example: Draw an array to find the missing number in the fact family.

$3 \times \underline{\ 8\ } = 24$

$\underline{\ 8\ } \times 3 = 24$

$24 \div 3 = \underline{\ 8\ }$

$24 \div \underline{\ 8\ } = 3$

Draw an array to find the missing number in the fact family.

$4 \times \underline{\hspace{1.5cm}} = 36$

$\underline{\hspace{1.5cm}} \times 4 = 36$

$36 \div 4 = \underline{\hspace{1.5cm}}$

$36 \div \underline{\hspace{1.5cm}} = 4$

Solve It Two Ways!

NAME: _____ **DATE:** _____

 **DIRECTIONS:** Show two ways to solve the problem.

1. Margaret has 32 stickers. She gives 4 stickers to each friend. How many friends will get stickers? Write multiplication and division equations to show the problem.

Strategy 1

Strategy 2

2. Which strategy do you think is better? Explain your reasoning.

_____

_____

_____

© Shell Education

NAME: _____ DATE: _____

DIRECTIONS: Read and solve the problem.

Kim and Kevin are practicing their multiplication and division facts. Kim tells Kevin to find all the fact families he knows with the product 24. Kevin writes 4 fact families. What fact families did Kevin write?

1. Write the fact families with the product 24.

_____ × _____ = _____	_____ × _____ = _____
_____ × _____ = _____	_____ × _____ = _____
_____ ÷ _____ = _____	_____ ÷ _____ = _____
_____ ÷ _____ = _____	_____ ÷ _____ = _____
_____ × _____ = _____	_____ × _____ = _____
_____ × _____ = _____	_____ × _____ = _____
_____ ÷ _____ = _____	_____ ÷ _____ = _____
_____ ÷ _____ = _____	_____ ÷ _____ = _____

2. Choose one fact family you wrote. Draw a picture to show the fact family.

Think About It!

NAME: _____ **DATE:** _____

DIRECTIONS: Think about the problem. Then, answer the questions.

Use two of the numbers to complete the division fact.

21   7   24

3

$$\boxed{} \div \boxed{} = 3$$

1. What information is given?

_____

_____

_____

2. What strategy can you use to solve the problem?

_____

_____

_____

_____

NAME: _____ **DATE:** _____

DIRECTIONS: Read and solve each problem.

Problem 1: Use two of the numbers to complete the division fact.

21   3   24   7

$\boxed{} \div \boxed{} = 3$

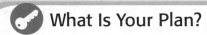

? What Do You Know?

⚷ What Is Your Plan?

💡 Solve the Problem!

_____ ÷ _____ = 3

🔍 Look Back and Explain!

Problem 2: Use two of the numbers to complete the division fact.

40   56   5   8

$\boxed{} \div \boxed{} = 8$

? What Do You Know?

⚷ What Is Your Plan?

💡 Solve the Problem!

_____ ÷ _____ = 8

🔍 Look Back and Explain!

Visualize It!

NAME: _____ **DATE:** _____

DIRECTIONS:
Look at the example. Then, solve the problem by completing the table.

Example:

Double (×2)	Double Double (×4)	Double Double Double (×8)
2 × 5 = ? Since, 2 × 5 = <u>10</u>, then <u>10</u> ÷ <u>2</u> = <u>5</u> and <u>10</u> ÷ <u>5</u> = <u>2</u>.	4 × 6 = ? 2 × <u>6</u> = <u>12</u> 2 × <u>12</u> = <u>24</u> Since, 4 × 6 = <u>24</u>, then <u>24</u> ÷ <u>4</u> = <u>6</u> and <u>24</u> ÷ <u>6</u> = <u>4</u>.	8 × 7 = ? 2 × <u>7</u> = <u>14</u> 2 × <u>14</u> = <u>28</u> 2 × <u>28</u> = <u>56</u> Since, 8 × 7 = <u>56</u>, then <u>56</u> ÷ <u>8</u> = <u>7</u> and <u>56</u> ÷ <u>7</u> = <u>8</u>.

Double (×2)	Double Double (×4)	Double Double Double (×8)
2 × 6 = ? Since, 2 × 6 = ____ , then ___ ÷ ___ = ___ and ___ ÷ ___ = ___.	4 × 8 = ? 2 × ____ = ____ 2 × ____ = ____ Since, 4 × 8 = ____ , then ___ ÷ ___ = ___ and ___ ÷ ___ = ___.	8 × 6 = ? 2 × ____ = ____ 2 × ____ = ____ 2 × ____ = ____ Since, 8 × 6 = ____ , then ___ ÷ ___ = ___ and ___ ÷ ___ = ___.

NAME: _____ DATE: _____

DIRECTIONS: Look at the first strategy. Then, solve the problem a different way.

1. There are 42 cans of green beans at the grocery store. There are 6 rows of canned green beans. How many cans of green beans are in each row?

- - - - (Strategy 1) -

$42 \div 6 = \boxed{}$

$6 \times \boxed{} = 42$

I know that 6 rows of 6 is 36.

$6 \times 6 = 36$

I will add one more row of 6.

$36 + 6 = 42$

$42 \div 6 = 7$

- - - - (Strategy 2) -

2. Which strategy do you think is easier? Explain your reasoning.

_____

_____

_____

Challenge Yourself!

NAME: _____ **DATE:** _____

DIRECTIONS: Read and solve the problem.

Carlos wants to put the pictures from his vacation in a scrapbook. The scrapbook holds 50 pictures. Carlos arranged his pictures on his desk in 9 rows with 6 in each row. Will all of Carlos's pictures fit in the scrapbook?

1. Draw a picture to show how many pictures Carlos has.

2. Will there be any pictures left over? Explain how you know.

_____

_____

_____

_____

NAME: _____ DATE: _____

 DIRECTIONS: Think about the problem. Then, answer the questions.

Meg's class is playing a game. The teacher divides the class into 5 groups with 6 students in each group. How many students are in the class?

1. What information is given?

_____

_____

2. What fact family will help you solve the problem?

_____

_____

_____

_____

Solve It!

NAME: _____ **DATE:** _____

DIRECTIONS: Read and solve each problem.

Problem 1: Meg's class is playing a game. The teacher divides the class into 5 groups with 6 students in each group. How many students are in the class?

? What Do You Know?

🔑 What Is Your Plan?

💡 Solve the Problem!

🔍 Look Back and Explain!

Problem 2: The class wants to play the game again. Meg's teacher invites another class to join them. She divides the students into 9 equal groups. There are 63 students in all. How many students are in each group?

? What Do You Know?

🔑 What Is Your Plan?

💡 Solve the Problem!

🔍 Look Back and Explain!

NAME: _____ DATE: _____

 **DIRECTIONS:** Look at the example. Then, solve the problem by drawing a picture.

Example: Diana baked 24 muffins for a bake sale. She put the muffins on 6 plates. Each plate has the same number of muffins. How many muffins are on each plate?

$$6 \times \underline{4} = 24$$

Diana also baked 28 cookies. She put the cookies into 4 bags. Each bag has the same number of cookies. How many cookies are in each bag?

$$4 \times \underline{\hspace{1cm}} = 28$$

NAME: _____ **DATE:** _____

DIRECTIONS: Show two ways to solve the problem.

1. Thomas invites 5 friends to the arcade. He has a total of 40 tokens. He gives each friend an equal number of tokens. How many tokens does each friend get?

· · · · · Strategy 1 ·

· · · · · Strategy 2 ·

2. Which strategy do you like better? Explain your reasoning.

_____

_____

_____

NAME: _____ **DATE:** _____

DIRECTIONS: Read and solve the problem.

Dolly's Pie Shop sells pieces of pie. Each pie is cut into 6 pieces. Sam bought 6 pies. Nine people will share them. How many pieces of pie will each person get?

Challenge Yourself!

1. How many pieces of pie does Sam buy? Draw a picture to show your answer.

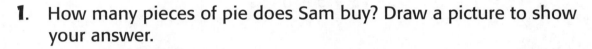

2. What is the solution to the problem? Explain your reasoning.

_____

_____

_____

_____

© Shell Education

#51615—180 Days of Problem Solving

Think About It!

NAME: _____ **DATE:** _____

DIRECTIONS: Think about the problem. Then, answer the questions.

Nick set up a lemonade stand. He spent $5 buying supplies. He charged $2 per glass and made $15 total. How many glasses of lemonade did he sell? Choose the equation that shows how to solve the problem.

A. $2 \times 5 + g = 15$	**C.** $15 - 5 = 2 + g$
B. $2 \times g - 5 = 15$	**D.** $15 \div 5 + g = 2$

1. What information is given?

_____

_____

2. What does the letter g stand for?

_____

_____

NAME: _____ **DATE:** _____

DIRECTIONS: Read and solve each problem.

Problem 1: Nick set up a lemonade stand. He spent $5 buying supplies. He charged $2 per glass and earned $15 total. How many glasses of lemonade did he sell? Choose the equation that shows how to solve the problem.

A. $2 \times 5 + g = 15$

B. $2 \times g - 5 = 15$

C. $15 - 5 = 2 + g$

D. $15 \div 5 + g = 2$

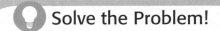 What Do You Know?

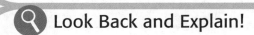 What Is Your Plan?

💡 Solve the Problem!

🔍 Look Back and Explain!

Problem 2: Nick had a car wash. He charged $10 for trucks and $5 for cars. He washed 4 trucks and earned $60 total. How many cars did he wash? Choose the equation that shows how to solve the problem.

A. $(4 \times 10) + (5 \times c) = 60$

B. $60 \div (4 \times 10) = c$

C. $(4 \times 10) - (5 \times c) = 60$

D. $c + 10 \times (4 \times 5) = 60$

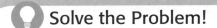 What Do You Know?

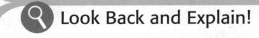 What Is Your Plan?

💡 Solve the Problem!

🔍 Look Back and Explain!

Visualize It!

NAME: _____ **DATE:** _____

DIRECTIONS: Look at the examples. Then, solve the problems.

Example: Heather has 32 marbles. Carol has 12 less. How many marbles do they have in all?

32

| 12 | M |

___32___ – ___12___ = ___20___

___32___ + ___20___ = ___52___ marbles

Evan has 14 pencils. Chris has 5 less. How many pencils do they have in all?

14

| 5 | P |

_____ – _____ = _____

_____ + _____ = _____ pencils

NAME: _____ **DATE:** _____

DIRECTIONS: Show two ways to solve the problem.

1. Jacob earned $30 for doing chores. He gives some of the money to his sister and buys a toy that costs $13. He has $7 left. How much money did he give to his sister?

Strategy 1

Strategy 2

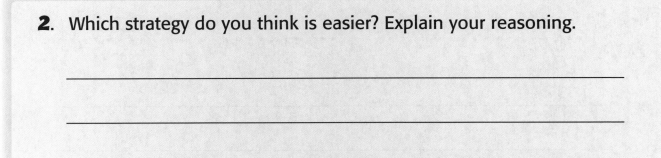

2. Which strategy do you think is easier? Explain your reasoning.

_____

_____

_____

Challenge Yourself!

NAME: _____ **DATE:** _____

DIRECTIONS: Read and solve the problem.

Emily wants to buy a new bike. The bike costs $225. She gets an allowance of $10 a week and has been saving for 7 weeks. She also earned $112 for babysitting. Does Emily have enough money to buy the bike?

1. How much money does Emily have? Write equations to show the answer.

_____

_____

_____

2. Solve the problem. Justify your answer.

_____

_____

_____

NAME: _____ **DATE:** _____

DIRECTIONS: Think about the problem. Then, answer the questions.

Hector is sharing a ham sandwich with his brother. He cut the sandwich into halves. How many equal parts are there?

1. What information is given?

_____

_____

_____

_____

2. What does the word *halves* mean?

_____

_____

_____

_____

Solve It!

NAME: _____ DATE: _____

DIRECTIONS: Read and solve each problem.

Problem 1: Hector is sharing a ham sandwich with his brother. He cut the sandwich into halves. How many equal parts are there?

 What Do You Know?

 What Is Your Plan?

Solve the Problem!

 Look Back and Explain!

Problem 2: Julia is sharing her granola bar with 2 friends. She cut the granola bar into thirds. How many equal parts are there?

 What Do You Know?

What Is Your Plan?

Solve the Problem!

 Look Back and Explain!

NAME: _____ **DATE:** _____

 DIRECTIONS: Look at the example. Then, solve the problem.

Visualize It!

Example: Write a fraction for the word problem. Then, draw a model to show the fraction.

Word problem	Fraction	Model
Samuel is eating pizza for lunch. The pizza is cut into 4 equal slices. He eats 1 slice.	$\frac{1}{4}$	

Write a fraction for the word problem. Then, draw a model to show the fraction.

Word problem	Fraction	Model
Amber is helping her mom bake corn bread. Her mom cuts the corn bread into 6 equal pieces. Amber eats 1 piece.		

NAME: _____ **DATE:** _____

DIRECTIONS: Show two ways to solve the problem.

1. Kacey and her two friends ate $\frac{3}{4}$ of a pie. They each ate the same amount. What fraction of the whole pie did each person eat?

> Strategy 1 ·

> Strategy 2 ·

2. Which strategy do you like better? Explain your reasoning.

_____

_____

_____

#51615—180 Days of Problem Solving

NAME: _____ **DATE:** _____

DIRECTIONS: Read and solve the problem.

Destiny and her dad bake a cake. Her dad cuts the cake into 6 equal pieces. Her family eats 3 pieces. She says, "We ate $\frac{1}{2}$ of the cake." Is Destiny correct?

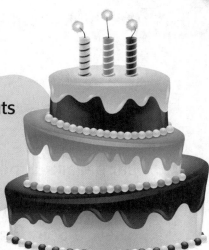

1. Draw a model to show the problem.

2. Do you agree with Destiny? Why or why not?

_____

_____

_____

_____

_____

Think About It!

NAME: _____ **DATE:** _____

DIRECTIONS: Think about the problem. Then, answer the questions.

Jane walks $\frac{1}{4}$ mile to school. Label each tick mark on the number line with a fraction. Draw a point on the number line to show $\frac{1}{4}$.

0   1

←———|————|————|————|————|———→

1. How many equal parts are in the whole?

_____

_____

2. What does the numerator tell you?

_____

_____

_____

NAME: _____ **DATE:** _____

 DIRECTIONS: Read and solve each problem.

Problem 1: Jane walks $\frac{1}{4}$ mile to school. Label each tick mark with a fraction. Draw a point on the number line to show $\frac{1}{4}$.

0   1
<----+----+----+----+----+----+----+----+---->

? **What Do You Know?**

🔑 **What Is Your Plan?**

💡 **Solve the Problem!**

🔍 **Look Back and Explain!**

Problem 2: Andrew ran $\frac{1}{6}$ mile on the track. Label each tick mark with a fraction. Draw a point on the number line to show $\frac{1}{6}$.

0   1
<----+----+----+----+----+----+----+---->

? **What Do You Know?**

🔑 **What Is Your Plan?**

💡 **Solve the Problem!**

🔍 **Look Back and Explain!**

Visualize It!

NAME: _____ **DATE:** _____

DIRECTIONS: Look at the example. Then, solve the problem.

Example: Label the tick marks to show the number line divided into thirds.

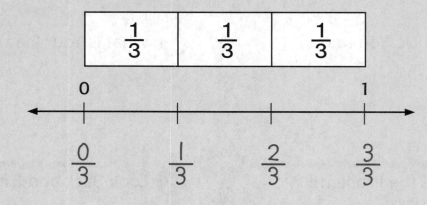

Label the tick marks to show the number line divided into fifths.

NAME: _____ **DATE:** _____

DIRECTIONS: Show two ways to solve the problem.

1. Travis has 7 baseball caps. One cap is blue. What fraction of his caps is blue?

· · · · Strategy 1 ·

Draw a picture to show the problem.

· · · · Strategy 2 ·

Show the fraction on the number line.

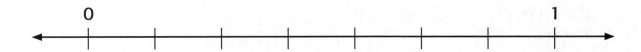

2. Which strategy do you like better? Explain your reasoning.

_____

_____

_____

Challenge Yourself!

NAME: _____ **DATE:** _____

DIRECTIONS: Read and solve the problem.

Draw a point and label each fraction on the number line.

$$\frac{1}{2} \qquad \frac{1}{3} \qquad \frac{1}{4}$$

0   1

←————————┼———————————————————————┼————————→

1. Which fraction is closest to 0? _____

2. Which fraction is exactly in the middle of 0 and 1? _____

3. Explain your strategy for labeling the fractions.

_____

_____

_____

_____

NAME: _____ DATE: _____

DIRECTIONS: Think about the problem. Then, answer the questions.

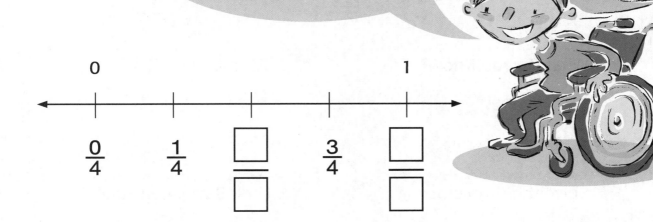

Find the missing fractions on the number line.

0   1

$\frac{0}{4}$ $\frac{1}{4}$ ⬚ $\frac{3}{4}$ ⬚

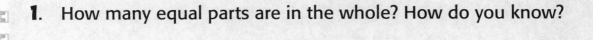

1. How many equal parts are in the whole? How do you know?

_____

_____

2. How can you find the numerators for the missing fractions?

_____

_____

_____

NAME: _____ DATE: _____

DIRECTIONS: Read and solve each problem.

Solve It!

Problem 1: Find the missing fractions on the number line.

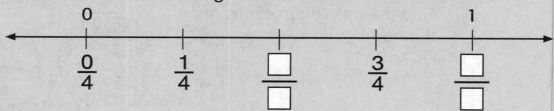

0 ⋮ ⋮ ⋮ ⋮ 1

$\frac{0}{4}$　$\frac{1}{4}$　$\frac{\Box}{\Box}$　$\frac{3}{4}$　$\frac{\Box}{\Box}$

? What Do You Know?

🔑 What Is Your Plan?

💡 Solve the Problem!

🔍 Look Back and Explain!

Problem 2: Find the missing fractions on the number line.

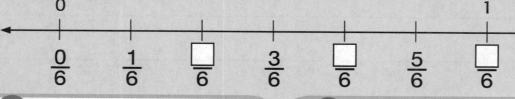

0 ⋮ ⋮ ⋮ ⋮ ⋮ ⋮ 1

$\frac{0}{6}$　$\frac{1}{6}$　$\frac{\Box}{6}$　$\frac{3}{6}$　$\frac{\Box}{6}$　$\frac{5}{6}$　$\frac{\Box}{6}$

? What Do You Know?

🔑 What Is Your Plan?

💡 Solve the Problem!

🔍 Look Back and Explain!

NAME: _____ DATE: _____

DIRECTIONS: Look at the example. Then, solve the problem.

Example: Label the tick marks to show the number line divided into thirds.

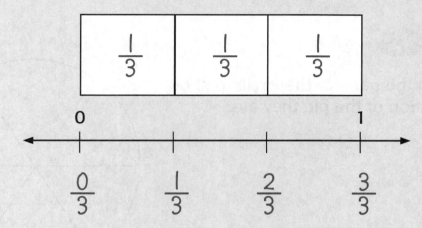

Label the tick marks to show the number line divided into eighths.

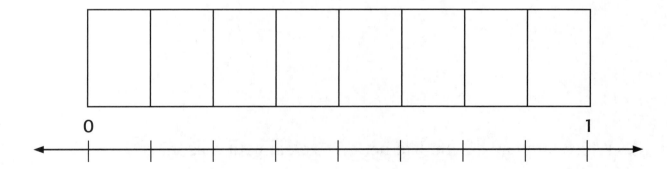

Solve It Two Ways!

NAME: _____ DATE: _____

DIRECTIONS: Show two ways to solve the problem.

1. Isaac and his friend ate some pie. Isaac ate $\frac{1}{6}$ of the pie. His friend ate $\frac{2}{6}$ of the pie. How much pie did they eat in all?

   Strategy 1

   Color in the parts of the circle to show the fraction of the pie they ate.

   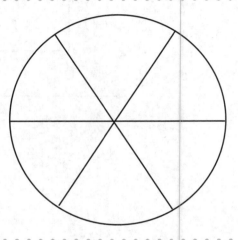

   Strategy 2

   Show the fraction of the pie they ate on the number line.

   0 1

2. Which strategy do you like better? Explain your reasoning.

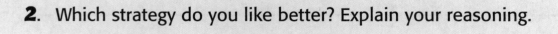

_____

_____

_____

NAME: _____ **DATE:** _____

DIRECTIONS: Read and solve the problem.

The number line shows the distance in miles between Tamika's home and her school. The bus picks her up at her house. It travels $\frac{2}{3}$ mile and picks up another student. Then, it travels another $\frac{2}{3}$ mile to pick up someone else. Draw a point on the number line to show how far the bus traveled. Label the missing fractions on the number line.

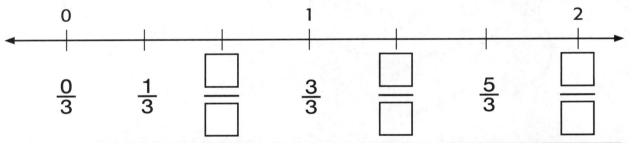

1. How far did the bus travel in total? Explain how you know.

_____

_____

_____

2. Did the bus travel more than 1 mile or less than 1 mile? Explain your answer.

_____

_____

_____

Think About It!

NAME: _____ DATE: _____

DIRECTIONS: Think about the problem. Then, answer the questions.

Look at the first circle. Then, color in the second circle to find the equivalent fraction.

$$\frac{1}{2} = \frac{\square}{4}$$

1. What does *equivalent fraction* mean?

_____

_____

2. How are the two circles the same?

_____

_____

3. How are the two circles different?

_____

_____

NAME: _____ **DATE:** _____

 **DIRECTIONS:** Read and solve each problem.

Solve It!

Problem 1: Look at the first circle. Then, color in the second circle to find the equivalent fraction.

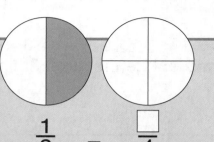

$$\frac{1}{2} = \frac{\square}{4}$$

? What Do You Know?

🔑 What Is Your Plan?

💡 Solve the Problem!

🔍 Look Back and Explain!

Problem 2: Look at the first rectangle. Then, color in the second rectangle to find the equivalent fraction.

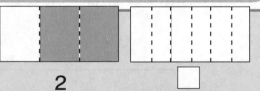

$$\frac{2}{3} = \frac{\square}{6}$$

? What Do You Know?

🔑 What Is Your Plan?

💡 Solve the Problem!

🔍 Look Back and Explain!

NAME: _____ **DATE:** _____

DIRECTIONS: Look at the example. Then, solve the problem.

Visualize It!

Example: Use the number lines below to find the equivalent fractions.

$$\frac{3}{4} = \frac{6}{8}$$

Use the number lines below to find the equivalent fractions.

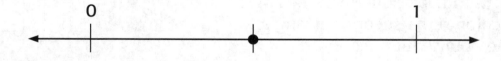

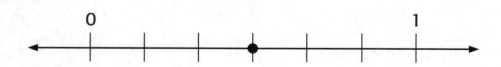

$$\frac{\square}{2} = \frac{\square}{6}$$

NAME: _____ DATE: _____

 DIRECTIONS: Show two ways to solve the problem.

1. Marcus read $\frac{5}{10}$ of a book. Juan read $\frac{7}{10}$ of the same book. Who read less? Circle the fraction that is less.

$$\frac{5}{10} \qquad\qquad\qquad \frac{7}{10}$$

Strategy 1

Draw a model to show your answer.

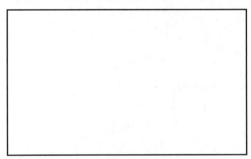 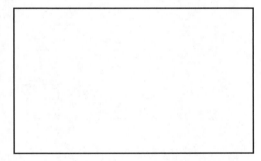

Strategy 2

Show your answer on the number line.

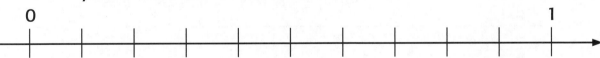

2. Which strategy do you like better? Explain your reasoning.

_____

_____

_____

NAME: _____ **DATE:** _____

DIRECTIONS: Read and solve the problem.

Label the four fractions on the number line. Then, write them in order from least to greatest.

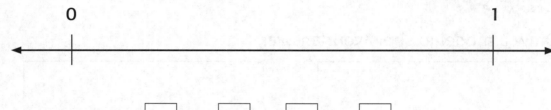

$$\frac{4}{7} \qquad \frac{3}{7} \qquad \frac{7}{7} \qquad \frac{1}{7}$$

0   1

$$\frac{\Box}{\Box} , \frac{\Box}{\Box} , \frac{\Box}{\Box} , \frac{\Box}{\Box}$$

1. Explain how you labeled each fraction on the number line.

   _____

   _____

   _____

2. Which fraction is the greatest? How do you know?

   _____

   _____

   _____

NAME: _____ DATE: _____

DIRECTIONS: Think about the problem. Then, answer the questions.

Kevin ate $\frac{1}{4}$ of his pizza. Monique ate $\frac{2}{8}$ of her pizza. Each pizza was the same size. Did they eat the same amount?

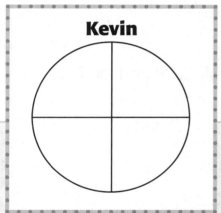

Kevin

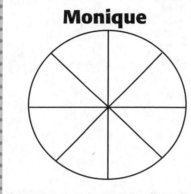

Monique

1. What information is given?

_____

_____

2. How can you compare the amount of pizza each person ate?

_____

_____

_____

Solve It!

NAME: _____ **DATE:** _____

DIRECTIONS: Read and solve each problem.

Problem 1: Kevin ate $\frac{1}{4}$ of his pizza. Monique ate $\frac{2}{8}$ of her pizza. Each pizza was the same size. Did they eat the same amount?

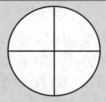

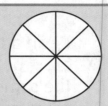

Kevin   **Monique**

 What Do You Know?

What Is Your Plan?

Solve the Problem!

Look Back and Explain!

Problem 2: Kai ate $\frac{2}{3}$ of his fruit bar. Lisa ate $\frac{5}{6}$ of her fruit bar. Each fruit bar was the same size. Did they eat the same amount?

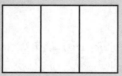

Kai   **Lisa**

What Do You Know?

What Is Your Plan?

Solve the Problem!

Look Back and Explain!

NAME: _____ **DATE:** _____

Visualize It!

DIRECTIONS: Look at the example. Then, solve the problem.

Example: Write the fractions in order from least to greatest.

$$\frac{4}{5} \qquad \frac{3}{7} \qquad \frac{2}{3}$$

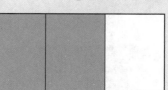

$$\frac{3}{7}, \quad \frac{2}{3}, \quad \frac{4}{5}$$

Write the fractions in order from least to greatest.

$$\frac{3}{4} \qquad\qquad \frac{5}{8} \qquad\qquad \frac{1}{3}$$

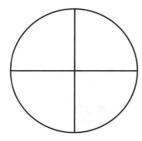 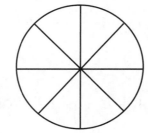 

$$\frac{\square}{\square}, \quad \frac{\square}{\square}, \quad \frac{\square}{\square}$$

Solve It Two Ways!

NAME: _____ DATE: _____

DIRECTIONS: Show two ways to solve the problem.

1. Robin and Kim each have a brownie. Robin cut her brownie into 2 equal pieces. She ate $\frac{1}{2}$ of her brownie. Kim cut her brownie into 6 equal pieces. Both girls ate the same amount. What fraction of her brownie did Kim eat?

$$\frac{1}{2} = \frac{\Box}{6}$$

Strategy 1

Strategy 2

2. Which strategy do you think is easier? Explain your reasoning.

_____

_____

_____

NAME: _____ DATE: _____

DIRECTIONS: Read and solve the problem.

Joey and Max each have a small pizza. Joey ate $\frac{1}{2}$ of his pizza. Max ate $\frac{4}{8}$ of his pizza. Max thinks he ate more pizza than Joey. Is Max correct?

1. Draw a model to show the problem.

2. Do you agree with Max? Explain your reasoning.

_____

_____

3. What fraction of the pizza does Max have left over? How do you know?

_____

_____

_____

Think About It!

NAME: _____ **DATE:** _____

DIRECTIONS: Think about the problem. Then, answer the questions.

Graph $\frac{5}{5}$ on the number line.

0   1

1. **What do you know about the fraction?**

    _____

    _____

    _____

2. **What fraction is each part of the number line equal to? How do you know?**

    _____

    _____

    _____

    _____

NAME: _____ **DATE:** _____

 DIRECTIONS: Read and solve each problem.

Solve It!

Problem 1: Graph $\frac{5}{5}$ on the number line.

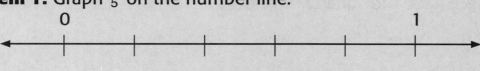

0   1

? What Do You Know?

⚷ What Is Your Plan?

💡 Solve the Problem!

🔍 Look Back and Explain!

Problem 2: Graph $\frac{10}{10}$ on the number line.

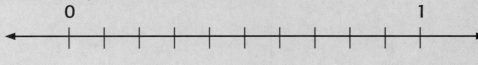

0   1

? What Do You Know?

⚷ What Is Your Plan?

💡 Solve the Problem!

🔍 Look Back and Explain!

NAME: _____ **DATE:** _____

DIRECTIONS: Look at the example. Then, solve the problem.

Example: Shade the squares to show $\frac{9}{4}$.

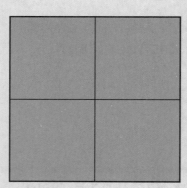 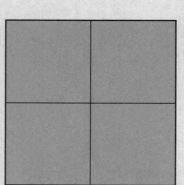 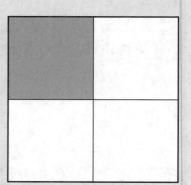

Shade the rectangles to show $\frac{7}{2}$.

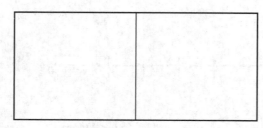

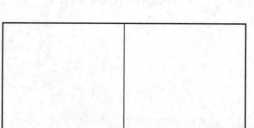

NAME: _____ **DATE:** _____

 **DIRECTIONS:** Show two ways to solve the problem.

1. Kyoko baked 2 trays of muffins. Each tray holds 6 muffins. She ate 1 muffin. What fraction of the muffins is left?

$\dfrac{}{6}$

Strategy 1

Use the model to show the answer.

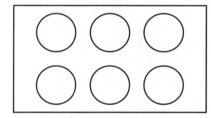 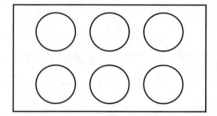

Strategy 2

Use the number line to show the answer.

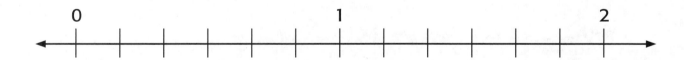

2. Which strategy do you like better? Explain your reasoning.

_____

_____

_____

NAME: _____ **DATE:** _____

DIRECTIONS: Read and solve the problem.

Nick bought two apples. One apple weighs $\frac{4}{3}$ pounds. The other apple weighs $\frac{7}{4}$ pounds. Which apple weighs more?

1. Draw a model to show your answer.

2. How do you know which apple weighs more? Explain your thinking.

_____

_____

_____

_____

NAME: _____ **DATE:** _____

DIRECTIONS: Think about the problem. Then, answer the questions.

Write fractions for the points on the number line. Then, circle the fraction that is greater.

0   1

1. How do you find the number of equal parts for the number line?

_____

_____

_____

2. How do you know if a fraction is greater?

_____

_____

_____

NAME: _____ **DATE:** _____

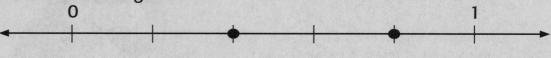

DIRECTIONS: Read and solve each problem.

Problem 1: Write fractions for the points on the number line. Then, circle the fraction that is greater.

0   1

 What Do You Know?

 What Is Your Plan?

Solve the Problem!

Look Back and Explain!

Problem 2: Write fractions for the points on the number line. Then, circle the fraction that is less.

0   1

 What Do You Know?

 What Is Your Plan?

Solve the Problem!

Look Back and Explain!

NAME: _____ **DATE:** _____

 **DIRECTIONS:** Look at the example. Then, solve the problem.

Example: Compare the fractions using >, <, or =. Draw a model to show your answer.

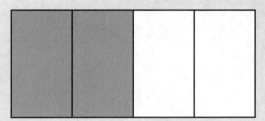

$\frac{2}{4}$

$\frac{2}{8}$

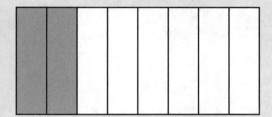

Compare the fractions using >, <, or =. Draw a model to show your answer.

$\frac{2}{3}$

$\frac{4}{6}$

Solve It Two Ways!

NAME: ______________________ **DATE:** ______________

DIRECTIONS: Show two ways to solve the problem.

1. Tomás ate $\frac{1}{4}$ of his sandwich. Alejandro's sandwich was the same size, but he ate $\frac{1}{2}$ of his. Who ate more of his sandwich?

Strategy 1

Strategy 2

2. Which strategy do you think is easier? Explain your reasoning.

____

____

____

NAME: _____ **DATE:** _____

DIRECTIONS: Read and solve the problem.

Lori is making a bag of trail mix. She uses a recipe to make one serving. Compare the fractions. Then, write them in order from least to greatest.

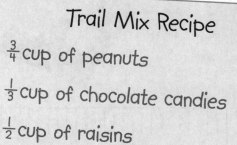

Trail Mix Recipe

$\frac{3}{4}$ cup of peanuts

$\frac{1}{3}$ cup of chocolate candies

$\frac{1}{2}$ cup of raisins

Challenge Yourself!

1. Draw a model to show your answer.

2. Explain how you ordered the fractions from least to greatest.

_____

_____

_____

Think About It!

NAME: _____ **DATE:** _____

DIRECTIONS: Think about the problem. Then, answer the questions.

The point on the number line shows the number of minutes it took Maria to do her math homework. How many minutes did Maria spend on her math homework?

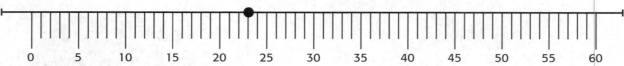

0   5   10   15   20   25   30   35   40   45   50   55   60

1. How many minutes are in an hour? How do you know?

_____

_____

_____

2. What can you count by to find the number of minutes?

_____

_____

_____

_____

NAME: _____ **DATE:** _____

DIRECTIONS: Read and solve the problem.

Problem: The point on the number line shows the number of minutes it took Maria to do her math homework. How many minutes did Maria spend on her math homework?

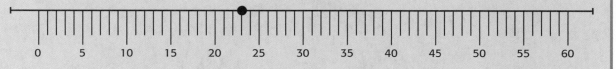

? What Do You Know?	**🔑** What Is Your Plan?

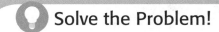 **💡** Solve the Problem!   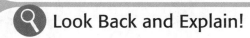 **🔍** Look Back and Explain!

NAME: _____ **DATE:** _____

DIRECTIONS: Look at the example. Then, solve the problem.

Example: What time is shown on the clock? Show how to count the minutes on the clock.

____6____ : ____12____

What time is shown on the clock? Show how to count the minutes on the clock.

_____ : _____

NAME: _____ **DATE:** _____

DIRECTIONS: Show two ways to solve the problem.

1. Alexis went to volleyball practice at 4:26 p.m. Show the time using the number line and the clock.

Strategy 1

Use the number line to show the answer.

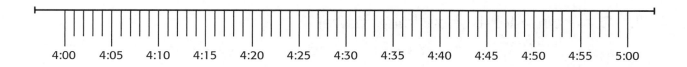

4:00   4:05   4:10   4:15   4:20   4:25   4:30   4:35   4:40   4:45   4:50   4:55   5:00

Strategy 2

Use the clock to show the answer.

2. Which strategy do you like better? Explain your reasoning.

_____

_____

_____

NAME: _____ **DATE:** _____

DIRECTIONS: Read and solve the problem.

The clock shows the time Angela gets to the movie theater. The movie starts at 6:15 p.m. In how many minutes will the movie begin?

1. Draw a model to show your answer.

2. Is your answer greater or less than $\frac{1}{2}$ hour? Explain your reasoning.

_____

_____

_____

_____

NAME: _____ **DATE:** _____

 DIRECTIONS: Think about the problem. Then, answer the questions.

The clock shows the time Linda walks home from school. It takes her 20 minutes to get home.

1. How do you know what the hour is on the clock?

_____

_____

2. How do you know the number of minutes on the clock?

_____

_____

3. Write a question that can be answered from this information.

_____

_____

DAY
2

NAME: _____ **DATE:** _____

 Read and solve each problem.

Solve It!

Problem 1: The clock shows the time Linda walks home from school. It takes her 20 minutes to get home. What time will Linda get home?

1:23

 What Do You Know?

 What Is Your Plan?

Solve the Problem!

Look Back and Explain!

Problem 2: The clock shows the time Linda starts reading her book. She reads for 15 minutes. What time will Linda finish reading her book?

2:19

 What Do You Know?

 What Is Your Plan?

 Solve the Problem!

 Look Back and Explain!

NAME: _____ **DATE:** _____

 DIRECTIONS: Look at the examples. Then, solve the problem.

Visualize It!

Example: Sara is making lasagna for dinner. She puts it in the oven at 5:30 p.m. She bakes the lasagna for 40 minutes. At what time does Sara take the lasagna out of the oven?

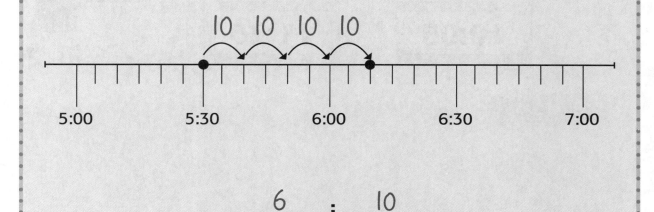

_____ 6 _____ : _____ 10 _____

Sara is making garlic bread. She puts it in the oven at 5:55 p.m. She bakes the bread for 20 minutes. At what time does Sara take the bread out of the oven?

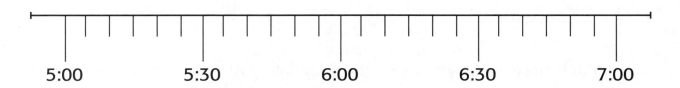

_____ : _____

NAME: _____ DATE: _____

DIRECTIONS: Show two ways to solve the problem.

1. Jackie has a violin lesson every Saturday morning. The start and end times of her lesson are shown on the clocks. How long is Jackie's lesson?

Start

10:05

End

11:20

Strategy 1

Strategy 2

2. Which strategy do you like better? Explain your reasoning.

_____

_____

_____

NAME: _____ DATE: _____

DIRECTIONS: Read and solve the problem.

Look at the morning schedule for Mr. Black's third-grade class. How many minutes longer is reading than writing?

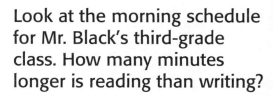

Morning Schedule

8:15–8:30	Welcome and Announcements
8:30–9:45	Reading
9:45–10:30	Writing
10:30–11:00	Spelling

1. Show how you found your answer.

2. How many hours and minutes have passed from the start to the end of the morning schedule? Explain your thinking.

_____

_____

_____

_____

Think About It!

NAME: _____ **DATE:** _____

DIRECTIONS: Think about the problem. Then, answer the questions.

Is it better to measure these items in grams or kilograms?

1. Which unit is smaller? _____

2. Which unit is larger? _____

3. Which two items weigh less? _____

   _____

4. Which two items weigh more? _____

   _____

NAME: _____ **DATE:** _____

 DIRECTIONS: Read and solve each problem.

Solve It!

Problem 1: Is it better to measure these items in grams or kilograms?

| paper clip | book | desk | pencil |

 What Do You Know?

 What Is Your Plan?

 Solve the Problem!

 Look Back and Explain!

Problem 2: Is it better to measure these items in milliliters or liters?

| juice box | pitcher of water | cup of milk | pot of soup |

 What Do You Know?

 What Is Your Plan?

 Solve the Problem!

 Look Back and Explain!

NAME: _____ **DATE:** _____

DIRECTIONS: Look at the example. Then, solve the problem.

Example: Estimate the mass of the objects. Write *about 1 gram* or *about 1 kilogram*.

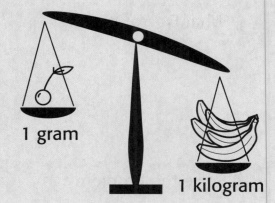

1 gram

1 kilogram

grape: _____about 1 gram_____

pineapple: _____about 1 kilogram_____

strawberry: _____about 1 gram_____

Estimate the liquid volume of the objects. Write *about 1 milliliter* or *about 1 liter*.

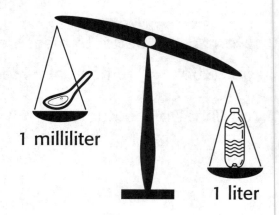

1 milliliter

1 liter

glass of lemonade: _____

bottle of water: _____

spoonful of medicine: _____

NAME: _____ **DATE:** _____

DIRECTIONS: Show two ways to solve the problem.

1. Reuben needs to estimate the weight of his laptop. He wants to compare its weight to the weight of his textbook. He knows his textbook weighs about 1 kilogram. How can he estimate the weight of his laptop? Use words or pictures to explain your strategies.

Strategy 1 ·

Strategy 2 ·

2. Which strategy do you think is better? Explain your reasoning.

_____

_____

_____

NAME: _____ DATE: _____

DIRECTIONS: Read and solve the problem.

Anne has a pitcher of iced tea that holds 6 liters. She wants to fill 4 glasses that each hold $1\frac{1}{2}$ liters. Does Anne have enough tea to fill the glasses?

1. Draw a picture to show the problem.

2. Is there enough iced tea to fill 4 glasses? Explain how you know.

_____

_____

_____

NAME: _____ **DATE:** _____

 DIRECTIONS: Think about the problem. Then, answer the questions.

Jane eats 9 cherries. Each one weighs 4 grams. What is the total weight of the cherries?

1. **What information is given?**

_____

_____

_____

2. **What operation will you use to solve the problem? Explain your reasoning.**

_____

_____

_____

_____

Solve It!

NAME: _____ DATE: _____

DIRECTIONS: Read and solve each problem.

Problem 1: Jane eats 9 cherries. Each one weighs 4 grams. What is the total weight of the cherries?

? What Do You Know?

🔑 What Is Your Plan?

💡 Solve the Problem!

🔍 Look Back and Explain!

Problem 2: There are 9 strawberries in a basket. The combined weight of the strawberries is 63 grams. How much does each strawberry weigh?

? What Do You Know?

🔑 What Is Your Plan?

💡 Solve the Problem!

🔍 Look Back and Explain!

#51615—180 Days of Problem Solving

NAME: _____ **DATE:** _____

 DIRECTIONS: Look at the example. Then, solve the problem.

Example: Mia's water bottle holds 840 milliliters. After soccer practice, she drinks 220 milliliters. How much water does she have left? Use the number line and write an equation to solve the problem.

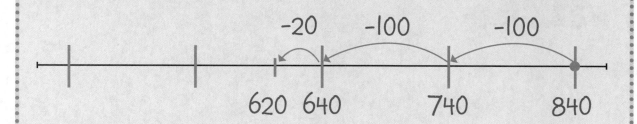

Equation: _840 – 220 = 620 milliliters_

Dan's sports bottle has 160 milliliters of water. He adds 320 milliliters more water. How much water is in the bottle now? Use the number line and write an equation to solve the problem.

Equation: _____

Solve It Two Ways!

NAME: _____ DATE: _____

DIRECTIONS: Show two ways to solve the problem.

1. The gas tank on Grandpa's truck holds 56 liters of gas. He just added 27 liters of gas to the tank and now it is full. How much gas was in the tank before he filled it up?

· · · · **Strategy 1** ·

· · · · **Strategy 2** ·

2. Which strategy do you think is better? Explain your reasoning.

_____

_____

_____

NAME: _____ DATE: _____

DIRECTIONS: Read and solve the problem.

Jayda loves to wear jewelry. She puts on a ring with a mass of 3 grams, 2 earrings with a mass of 1 gram each, 5 bracelets with a mass of 6 grams each, and a necklace with a mass of 10 grams. What is the total mass of Jayda's jewelry?

1. Show how you solved the problem.

2. Use words to explain how you found the total mass.

_____

_____

_____

Think About It!

NAME: _____ **DATE:** _____

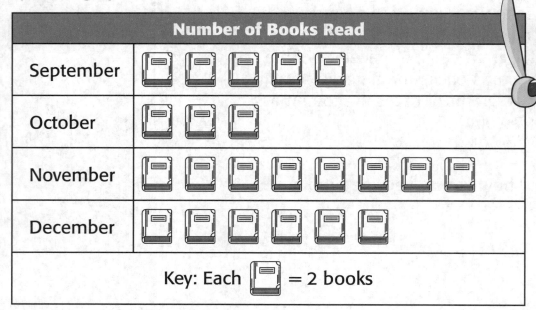

DIRECTIONS: Think about the problem. Then, answer the questions.

Ty keeps track of how many books he reads each month. Look at the picture graph.

Number of Books Read							
September	📖	📖	📖	📖	📖		
October	📖	📖	📖				
November	📖	📖	📖	📖	📖	📖	📖
December	📖	📖	📖	📖	📖	📖	

Key: Each 📖 = 2 books

1. How many books does each picture stand for?

_____

_____

2. Write a question that can be answered from the graph.

_____

_____

_____

_____

NAME: _____ DATE: _____

 DIRECTIONS: Read and solve the problem.

Solve It!

Problem: Ty keeps track of how many books he reads each month. Look at the picture graph. How many books did Ty read in October?

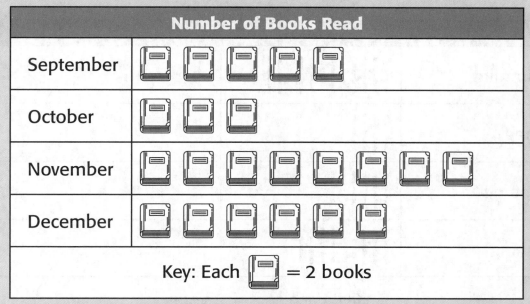

Number of Books Read	
September	📘 📘 📘 📘 📘
October	📘 📘 📘
November	📘 📘 📘 📘 📘 📘 📘 📘
December	📘 📘 📘 📘 📘 📘

Key: Each 📘 = 2 books

? **What Do You Know?**

🔑 **What Is Your Plan?**

💡 **Solve the Problem!**

🔍 **Look Back and Explain!**

Visualize It!

NAME: _____ DATE: _____

DIRECTIONS: Look at the example. Then, solve the problem.

Example: Count the number of tally marks and complete the picture graph.

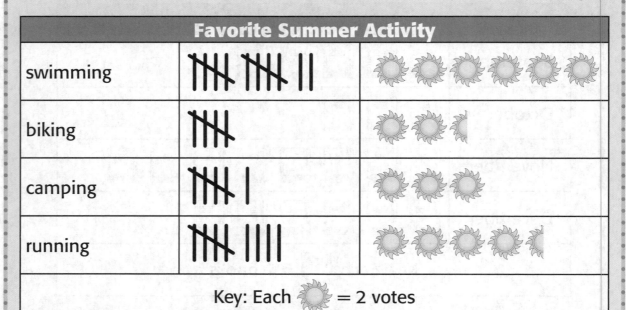

Favorite Summer Activity		
swimming	卌 卌 ‖	☀ ☀ ☀ ☀ ☀ ☀
biking	卌	☀ ☀ ◗
camping	卌 ‖	☀ ☀ ☀
running	卌 ‖‖‖	☀ ☀ ☀ ☀ ◗
Key: Each ☀ = 2 votes		

Count the number of tally marks and complete the picture graph.

Favorite Type of Cookies	
chocolate chip	卌 卌 卌 ‖
peanut butter	卌 卌
oatmeal raisin	卌 ‖
sugar cookie	卌 卌 卌 卌
Key: Each 🍪 = 4 votes	

NAME: _____ **DATE:** _____

 DIRECTIONS: Show two ways to solve the problem.

1. Look at the picture graph. How many more students voted for the zoo or park than both museums?

Favorite Field Trip	
zoo	🚌🚌🚌🚌
art museum	🚌🚌🚌
park	🚌🚌🚌🚌🚌🚌
symphony	🚌🚌
history museum	🚌🚌🚌

Key: Each 🚌 = 10 votes

Strategy 1

Strategy 2

2. Which strategy do you think is easier? Explain your reasoning.

_____

_____

_____

NAME: _____ DATE: _____

DIRECTIONS: Read and solve the problem.

The Lightning soccer team keeps track of the number of goals each player scores. Use this information to create a picture graph.

Title: _____	
Key: Each _____ = _____	

Lucy—6 goals

Marco—3 goals

Charlie—10 goals

David—9 goals

Julie—7 goals

Grace—5 goals

1. How many goals did the players score in all? Show how you found your answer.

2. How many more goals did the boys score than the girls? Explain how you found your answer.

_____

_____

_____

#51615—180 Days of Problem Solving

NAME: _____ DATE: _____

DIRECTIONS: Think about the problem. Then, answer the questions.

Perry took pictures each day on his vacation. Look at the bar graph. On which day did Perry take the fewest pictures?

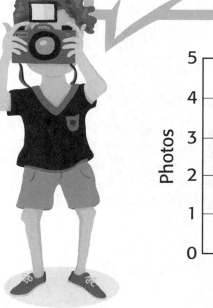

Family Vacation Photos

Photos

5	
4	
3	
2	
1	
0	

Monday Tuesday Wednesday Thursday

Days of the week

1. What does the graph show?

_____

_____

2. What does *fewest* mean?

_____

_____

NAME: _____ **DATE:** _____

Solve It!

DIRECTIONS: Read and solve the problem.

Problem: Perry took pictures each day on his vacation. Look at the bar graph. On which day did Perry take the fewest pictures?

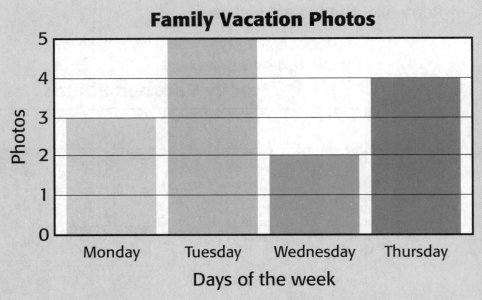

Family Vacation Photos

Photos

Days of the week

| ? | What Do You Know? |

| 🔑 | What Is Your Plan? |

| 💡 | Solve the Problem! |

| 🔍 | Look Back and Explain! |

 #51615—180 Days of Problem Solving

NAME: _____ **DATE:** _____

 DIRECTIONS: Look at the example. Then, solve the problem.

Example: A group of friends are comparing how long they have lived in their neighborhood. Look at the information in the table to complete the bar graph.

Name	Number of years
Esperanza	6
Adrian	1
Kenzie	8
Henry	4

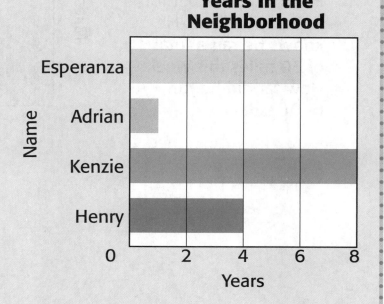

The friends also compared how many people are in their families. Look at the information in the table to complete the bar graph.

Name	Number of people
Esperanza	4
Adrian	5
Kenzie	6
Henry	3

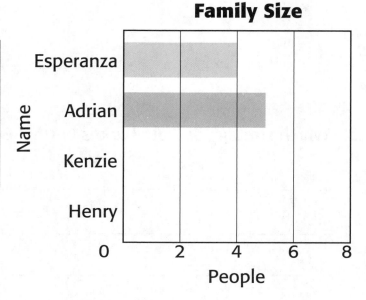

Solve It Two Ways!

NAME: _____ DATE: _____

Show two ways to solve the problem.

1. Luis keeps track of the distance he runs each day on a bar graph. He notices the bar for Tuesday is blank. He knows he ran a total of 30 miles this week. How far did he run on Tuesday?

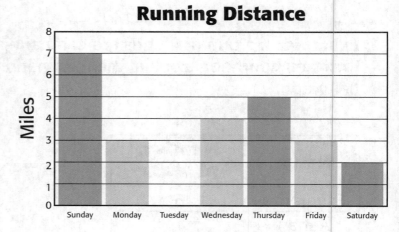

Running Distance

Miles

Days of the week

Strategy 1

Strategy 2

2. Which strategy do you think is better? Explain your reasoning.

_____

_____

_____

NAME: _____ DATE: _____

DIRECTIONS: Read and solve the problem.

The students in Mrs. Lin's third-grade class voted for their favorite flavor of ice cream. The results are shown in the table. Use this information to create a bar graph.

Flavor	Number of votes
chocolate	4
vanilla	3
strawberry	1
chocolate chip	8
cookies and cream	6

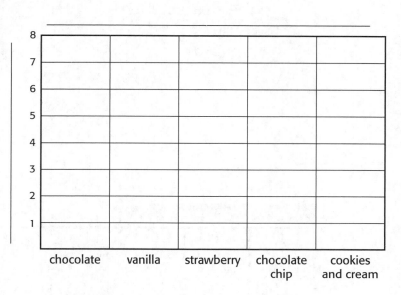

1. How many students are in Mrs. Lin's class? Show how you found your answer.

2. Write and solve a question that matches the data in your graph.

_____

_____

NAME: _____ DATE: _____

DIRECTIONS: Think about the problem. Then, answer the questions.

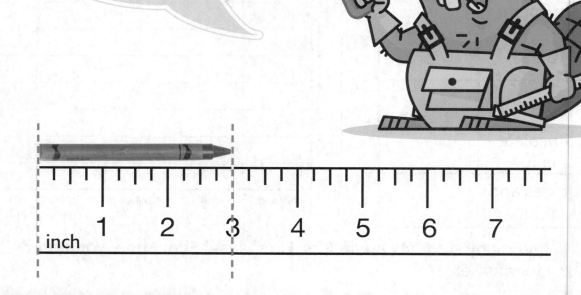

Use this ruler to measure the crayon to the nearest inch.

inch   1   2   3   4   5   6   7

1. What do the numbers on the ruler stand for?

   _____

   _____

2. What does *nearest inch* mean?

   _____

   _____

NAME: _____ DATE: _____

 DIRECTIONS: Read and solve each problem.

Problem 1: Use this ruler to measure the crayon to the nearest inch.

inch 1 2 3 4 5 6 7

? What Do You Know?

⚷ What Is Your Plan?

💡 Solve the Problem!

🔍 Look Back and Explain!

Problem 2: Use this ruler to measure the paperclip to the nearest half inch.

inch 1 2 3 4 5 6 7

? What Do You Know?

⚷ What Is Your Plan?

💡 Solve the Problem!

🔍 Look Back and Explain!

NAME: _____ DATE: _____

DIRECTIONS: Look at the example. Then, solve the problem.

Visualize It!

Example: A third-grade class measured the length of their shoes. Use the data in the table to complete the line plot. Draw an "X" for each length.

Length of shoe (inches)	Number of students
8	ℍℍ
10	‖
9	‖‖
$7\frac{1}{2}$	‖‖
$9\frac{1}{2}$	ℍℍ

Shoe Lengths

```
                    x               x
                    x         x     x
              x     x         x     x
              x     x         x     x     x
              x     x         x     x     x
    ---|-----|-----|-----|-----|-----|-----|---
       7    7½    8    8½    9    9½    10
```
Length in inches

The class also measured their shoelaces. Use the data in the table to complete the line plot. Draw an "X" for each length.

Length of shoelace (inches)	Number of students
27	‖‖
$26\frac{1}{4}$	ℍℍ
$27\frac{3}{4}$	‖‖
$27\frac{1}{4}$	‖
$26\frac{1}{2}$	ℍℍ ‖

Shoelance Lengths

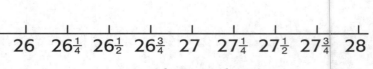

```
   ---|-----|-----|-----|-----|-----|-----|-----|-----|---
     26   26¼  26½  26¾   27   27¼  27½  27¾   28
```
Length in inches

NAME: _____ DATE: _____

DIRECTIONS: Show two ways to solve the problem.

1. Student 1 measured a pencil. She found that the pencil is $6\frac{1}{2}$ inches. Student 2 measured the same pencil. He found that the pencil is $5\frac{1}{2}$ inches. Look at the models. Which student measured the pencil correctly? Circle the correct model.

Student 1

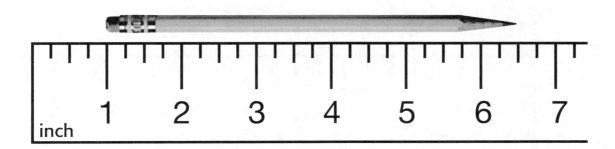

Student 2

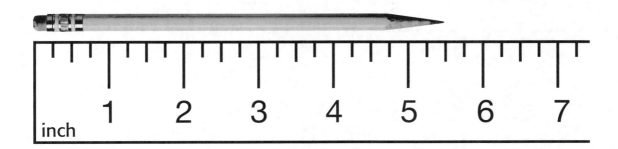

2. What mistake did the other student make? Explain your reasoning.

_____

_____

_____

NAME: _____ **DATE:** _____

DIRECTIONS: Read and solve the problem.

Use this ruler to measure each string to the nearest half inch.

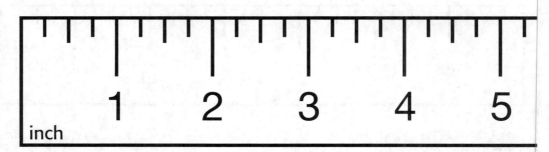

_____

_____

_____

_____

_____

_____

1. Create a line plot to show the data. Draw an "X" for each length.

2. Between which two inch-marks on the ruler is the shortest string?

_____

NAME: _____ **DATE:** _____

 DIRECTIONS: Think about the problem. Then, answer the questions.

What is the area of the shape?

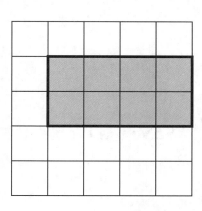

1. What does the word *area* mean?

   _____

   _____

   _____

2. How can you find the area of a shape?

   _____

   _____

   _____

NAME: _____ **DATE:** _____

DIRECTIONS: Read and solve each problem.

Problem 1: What is the area of the shape?

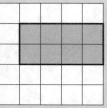

? What Do You Know?

🔑 What Is Your Plan?

💡 Solve the Problem!

🔍 Look Back and Explain!

Problem 2: What is the area of the shape?

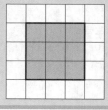

? What Do You Know?

🔑 What Is Your Plan?

💡 Solve the Problem!

🔍 Look Back and Explain!

NAME: _____ **DATE:** _____

 **DIRECTIONS:** Look at the example. Then, solve the problem.

Example: Draw a shape that has an area of 10 square units.

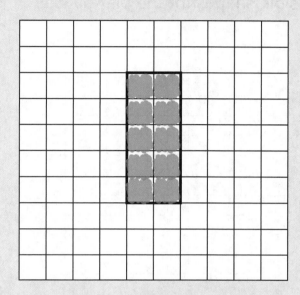

Draw a shape that has an area of 12 square units.

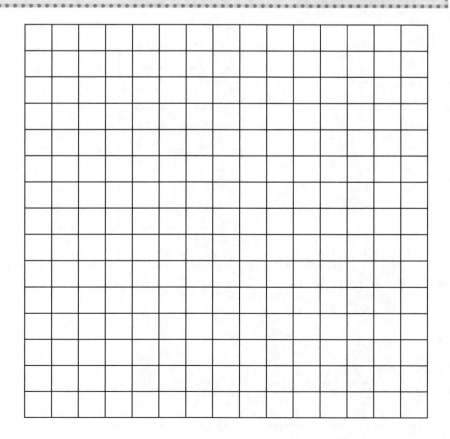

Solve It Two Ways!

NAME: _____ **DATE:** _____

DIRECTIONS: Show two ways to solve the problem.

1. Mr. Ricardo is making a play space for his dog. He wants the space to have an area of 24 square units. Draw two possible shapes for the play space.

Shape 1

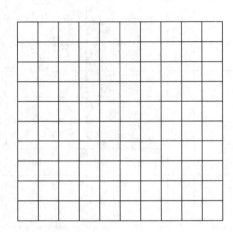

Shape 2

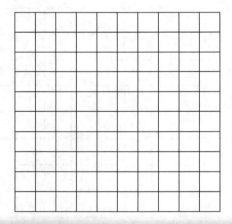

2. Which shape do you think is better for the play space? Explain your reasoning.

_____

_____

_____

NAME: _____ DATE: _____

DIRECTIONS: Read and solve the problem.

Elias wants to move the furniture in his bedroom. Draw the shapes to make all of the furniture fit in his bedroom.

bed = 18 square units

table = 4 square units

desk = 6 square units

dresser = 8 square units

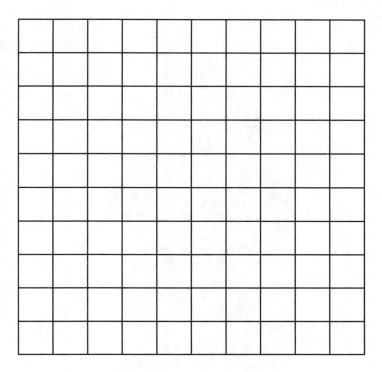

1. Does all of the furniture fit in the bedroom? Explain your answer.

_____

_____

_____

2. What is the total number of square units for all of the furniture? Explain how you found your answer.

_____

_____

_____

NAME: _____ DATE: _____

DIRECTIONS: Think about the problem. Then, answer the questions.

What is the area of the shape? Each unit square is 1 square inch.

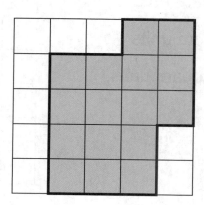

1. How can you find the area of the shape?

_____

_____

2. What unit is used to measure the area?

_____

_____

_____

NAME: _____ DATE: _____

 DIRECTIONS: Read and solve each problem.

Solve It!

Problem 1: What is the area of the shape?
Each unit square is 1 square inch.

? What Do You Know?

🔑 What Is Your Plan?

💡 Solve the Problem!

🔍 Look Back and Explain!

Area = _____ square inches

Problem 2: What is the area of the shape?
Each unit square is 1 square foot.

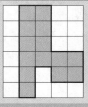

? What Do You Know?

🔑 What Is Your Plan?

💡 Solve the Problem!

🔍 Look Back and Explain!

Area = _____ square inches

NAME: _____ **DATE:** _____

DIRECTIONS: Look at the example. Then, solve the problem.

Example: Draw a shape that has an area of 8 square meters. Each unit square is 1 square meter.

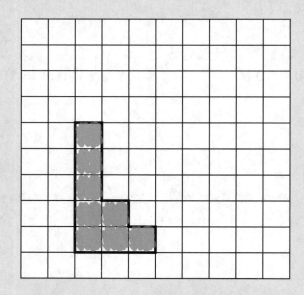

Draw a shape that has an area of 16 square centimeters. Each unit square is 1 square centimeter.

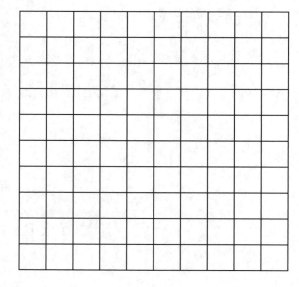

NAME: _____ **DATE:** _____

 DIRECTIONS: Show two ways to solve the problem.

1. Mrs. Evans wants to put a new tile floor in her bathroom. The bathroom floor is 36 square feet. Draw two possible shapes for the bathroom floor.

Shape 1

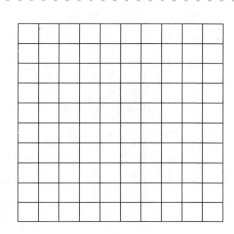

Shape 2

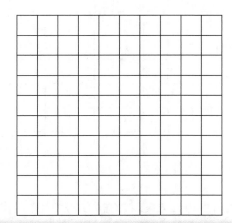

2. Which shape do you think is better for a bathroom floor? Explain your reasoning.

_____

_____

_____

NAME: _____ **DATE:** _____

DIRECTIONS: Read and solve the problem.

Design your dream backyard. Draw and label 5 or more shapes to show what you want in your backyard. Each square unit is 1 square foot.

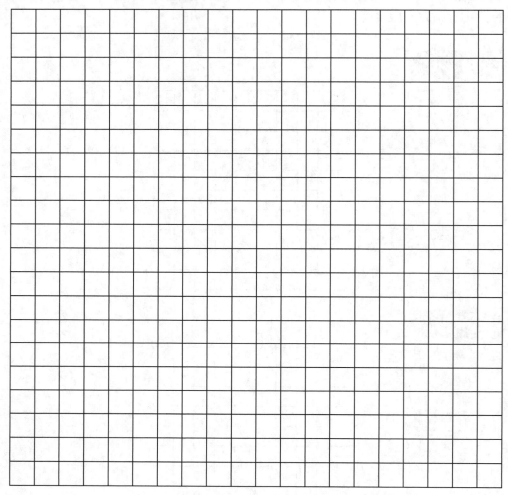

What is the total number of square feet for all of the shapes you drew? Show how you found your answer.

NAME: _____ **DATE:** _____

 DIRECTIONS: Think about the problem. Then, answer the questions.

Write a multiplication equation to find the area of the rectangle.

3 units

6 units

1. What information is given?

_____

_____

_____

2. How can you find the area of a rectangle using multiplication?

_____

_____

_____

_____

Solve It!

NAME: _____ **DATE:** _____

DIRECTIONS: Read and solve each problem.

Problem 1: Write a multiplication equation to find the area of the rectangle.

3 units

6 units

? What Do You Know?

⚷ What Is Your Plan?

💡 Solve the Problem!

_____ × _____ = _____

🔍 Look Back and Explain!

Problem 2: Write a multiplication equation to find the area of the rectangle.

2 units

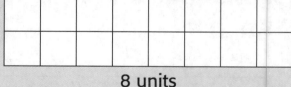

8 units

? What Do You Know?

⚷ What Is Your Plan?

💡 Solve the Problem!

_____ × _____ = _____

🔍 Look Back and Explain!

NAME: _____ DATE: _____

 DIRECTIONS: Look at the example. Then, solve the problem.

Example: Lee is making a quilt with her grandmother. Each square is 6 inches long and 6 inches wide. What is the area of each square? Draw a picture and write an equation to solve the problem.

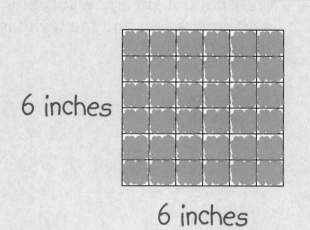

6 inches

6 inches

_____6_____ × _____6_____ = _____36_____ square inches

Lee's quilt will be 5 feet long and 3 feet wide. What is the area of the quilt? Draw a picture and write an equation to solve the problem.

_____ × _____ = _____ square feet

NAME: _____ DATE: _____

DIRECTIONS: Show two ways to solve the problem.

1. Mrs. Choi bought a new rug. She knows the area of the rug is 40 square feet and the width is 5 feet. What is the length of the rug?

Strategy 1 ·

Strategy 2 ·

2. Which strategy do you think is easier? Explain your reasoning.

_____

_____

_____

NAME: _____ **DATE:** _____

DIRECTIONS: Read and solve the problem.

Marcel is planting grass seed in a rectangular space in his backyard. The space is 9 meters long and 7 meters wide. He knows a bag of grass seed will cover 10 square meters. How many bags of grass seed will he need to cover the space in his backyard?

1. Draw a picture to show the space in Marcel's backyard.

2. How many bags will Marcel need? Explain how you found your answer.

_____

_____

_____

Think About It!

NAME: _____ DATE: _____

DIRECTIONS: Think about the problem. Then, answer the questions.

Mark wants to find the perimeter of his rectangular desktop. The length measures 8 inches and the width measures 5 inches. What is the perimeter of his desk?

1. How is perimeter different from area?

_____

_____

_____

_____

2. How can you find the perimeter of the desk?

_____

_____

_____

_____

_____

NAME: _____ **DATE:** _____

 DIRECTIONS: Read and solve each problem.

Problem 1: Mark wants to find the perimeter of his rectangular desktop. The length measures 8 inches and the width measure 5 inches. What is the perimeter of his desk?

 What Do You Know?

What Is Your Plan?

Solve the Problem!

Look Back and Explain!

Problem 2: Susan wants to put a fence around her garden. The picture shows the length of each side of her garden. How many feet of fencing should she buy?

4 ft.
4 ft.
7 ft.
3 ft.
7 ft.
3 ft.

 What Do You Know?

What Is Your Plan?

Solve the Problem!

Look Back and Explain!

Solve It!

NAME: _____ **DATE:** _____

Visualize It!

DIRECTIONS: Look at the example. Then, solve the problem.

Example: The perimeter of this shape is 20 meters. Find the length of side *h*.

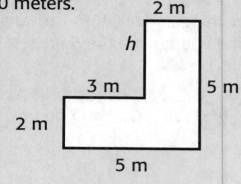

2 m

h

3 m

5 m

2 m

5 m

Step 1: __2__ + __5__ + __5__ + __2__ + __3__ = __17__

Step 2: __20__ – __17__ = __3__

Step 3: *h* = __3 meters__

The perimeter of the figure is 36 inches. Find the length of side *j*.

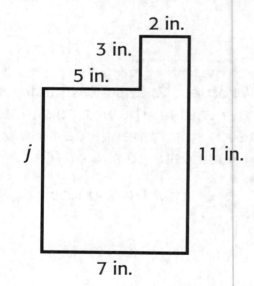

2 in.

3 in.

5 in.

j

11 in.

7 in.

Step 1: _____ + _____ + _____ + _____ + _____ = _____

Step 2: _____ – _____ = _____

Step 3: *j* = _____

NAME: _____ **DATE:** _____

DIRECTIONS: Show two ways to solve the problem.

1. Mrs. Norris is putting a border around the bulletin board in her classroom. The bulletin board is 8 feet long and 4 feet wide. She has 30 feet of border material. Does Mrs. Norris have enough for the bulletin? If so, how much is left over? If not, how much more does she need?

····· Strategy 1 ·······································

····· Strategy 2 ·······································

2. Which strategy do you think is easier? Explain your reasoning.

_____

_____

_____

Challenge Yourself!

NAME: _____ **DATE:** _____

DIRECTIONS: Read and solve the problem.

The two rectangles have the same perimeter. The area of the second rectangle is 16 square centimeters. What are the lengths of the sides of the second rectangle?

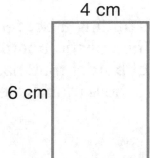

4 cm

6 cm

1. How did you find the lengths of the sides of the second rectangle? Explain how you found your answer.

_____

_____

_____

_____

2. Which rectangle has a greater area? How do you know?

_____

_____

_____

_____

NAME: _____ DATE: _____

DIRECTIONS: Think about the problem. Then, answer the questions.

Draw a quadrilateral that has only 1 pair of opposite sides that are parallel. Circle the name of the quadrilateral.

pentagon   trapezoid   triangle   rectangle

1. What information is given?

_____

_____

_____

2. What does *parallel* mean?

_____

_____

_____

Solve It!

NAME: _____ DATE: _____

 DIRECTIONS: Read and solve each problem.

Problem 1: Draw a quadrilateral that has only 1 pair of opposite sides that are parallel. Circle the name of the quadrilateral.

pentagon   trapezoid   triangle   rectangle

 What Do You Know?

What Is Your Plan?

 Solve the Problem!

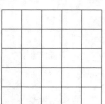

Look Back and Explain!

Problem 2: Draw a quadrilateral that has 2 pairs of equal sides and 4 right angles. Circle the name of the quadrilateral.

hexagon   parallelogram   rectangle   rhombus

 What Do You Know?

 What Is Your Plan?

 Solve the Problem!

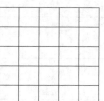

Look Back and Explain!

NAME: _____ **DATE:** _____

 DIRECTIONS: Look at the example. Then, solve the problem.

Example: Compare and contrast the two quadrilaterals. Be sure to include information about the lengths of their sides, types of angles, and number of parallel sides.

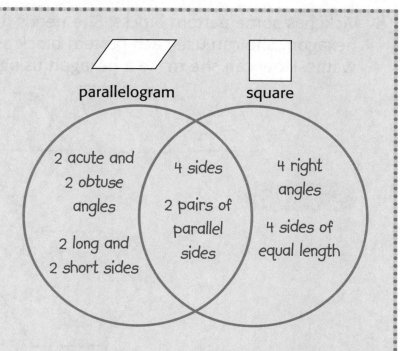

parallelogram   square

2 acute and 2 obtuse angles

2 long and 2 short sides

4 sides

2 pairs of parallel sides

4 right angles

4 sides of equal length

Compare and contrast the two quadrilaterals. Be sure to include information about the lengths of their sides, types of angles, and number of parallel sides.

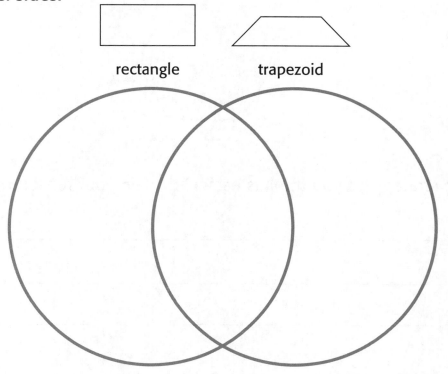

rectangle   trapezoid

Solve It Two Ways!

NAME: _____ **DATE:** _____

DIRECTIONS: Show two ways to solve the problem.

1. Vicki has some pattern blocks. She needs to use them to make a hexagon. She can use each pattern block as many times as she wants. How can she make a hexagon using these shapes?

· · · · Strategy 1 ·

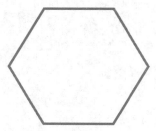

· · · · Strategy 2 ·

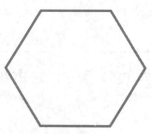

2. Which strategy do you think is easier? Explain your reasoning.

_____

_____

_____

NAME: _____ DATE: _____

DIRECTIONS: Read and solve the problem.

Danielle wants to compare and contrast shapes with right angles and shapes that have opposite sides equal in length. She needs to draw the shapes in the correct section of the Venn diagram. Draw the shapes to complete the diagram.

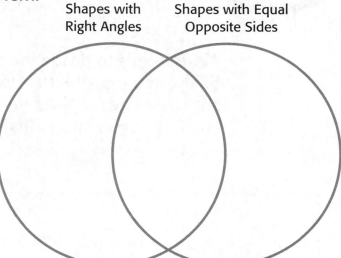

Shapes with Right Angles   Shapes with Equal Opposite Sides

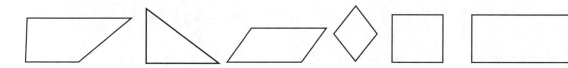

1. What shapes have right angles?

   _____

   _____

2. What shapes have opposite sides equal in length?

   _____

   _____

3. Look at the shape below. Can you draw this shape in the Venn diagram? Why or why not?

   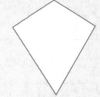   _____

   _____

Think About It!

NAME: _____ **DATE:** _____

DIRECTIONS: Think about the problem. Then, answer the questions.

Alexis needs to divide the shapes below into equal parts. How can she draw lines to divide a square and a hexagon into sixths?

1. What information is given?

_____

_____

_____

_____

2. How many equal parts will each shape have? How do you know?

_____

_____

_____

_____

NAME: _____ DATE: _____

 DIRECTIONS: Read and solve each problem.

Solve It!

Problem 1: Alexis needs to divide the shapes into equal parts. How can she draw lines to divide a square and a hexagon into sixths?

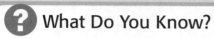 What Do You Know?

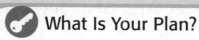 What Is Your Plan?

Solve the Problem!

Look Back and Explain!

Problem 2: How can Alexis draw lines to divide a circle and a rectangle into eighths?

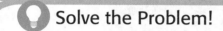 What Do You Know?

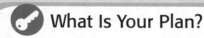 What Is Your Plan?

Solve the Problem!

Look Back and Explain!

NAME: _____ DATE: _____

DIRECTIONS: Look at the example. Then, solve the problem.

Example: Monique cut her sandwich into 2 equal pieces and ate 1 piece. Jessie cut her sandwich into 4 equal pieces and ate 3 pieces. Who ate more of her sandwich?

Monique   Jessie

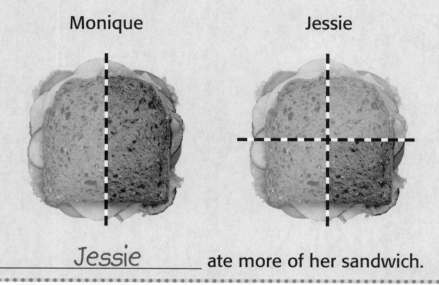

_____ _Jessie_ _____ ate more of her sandwich.

Monique cut a pie into 3 equal pieces and ate 1 piece. Jessie cut another pie into 8 equal pieces and ate 2 pieces. Who ate more pie?

Monique   Jessie

_____ ate more pie.

NAME: _____ DATE: _____

DIRECTIONS: Show two ways to solve the problem.

1. Mrs. Silva's construction company wants to sell some land. Plan A charges $3,000 for $\frac{1}{6}$ of the land. Plan B charges $5,000 for $\frac{1}{4}$ of the land. Which plan will make the company the most money if they sell all of the land?

..... Strategy 1 ....

..... Strategy 2 ....

2. Which strategy do you think is easier? Explain your reasoning.

_____

_____

_____

Challenge Yourself!

NAME: _____ DATE: _____

DIRECTIONS: Read and solve the problem.

Dean is making a poster for his science project. He cuts a sheet of paper into eight equal pieces to make a border around the outside of the poster. Show three ways Dean can cut the paper.

1. What fraction of the whole is each part? _____

2. Does each part have the same area? Explain how you know.

_____

_____

_____

_____

_____

ANSWER KEY

Week 1: Day 1 (page 13)

1. Possible answer: To make the greatest number, I should put the greatest digit in the thousands place. Then, the digits should decrease in order for the hundreds, tens, and ones place values.
2. The 2 should be in the ones place; it is the digit with the least value.

Week 1: Day 2 (page 14)

1. 7,642; To make the greatest number, the greatest digit should go in the thousands place. Digits should be in order from greatest to least.
2. 1,359; To make the least number, the least digit should go in the thousands place. Digits should be in order from least to greatest.

Week 1: Day 3 (page 15)

1. 620
2. 600

Week 1: Day 4 (page 16)

1. Lucy might be thinking of 195, 196, 197, 198, 199, 200, 201, 202, 203, or 204.
2. Possible answer: Using a number line is easier for me because it helps me see where the nearest 10 is located.

Week 1: Day 5 (page 17)

1. 9,316
2. 9,320
3. 9,300

Week 2: Day 1 (page 18)

1. The pattern is counting by tens.
2. Possible answer: I need to find the pattern, so I can figure out what the last two numbers are on the number line.

Week 2: Day 2 (page 19)

1. 93, 103; number line shows a pattern that is increasing; count to see by how much each number increases; pattern is increasing by 10
2. 138, 142; number line shows a pattern that is increasing; count to see by how much each number increases; pattern is increasing by 4

Week 2: Day 3 (page 20)

1.

Rule: add 50	
In	Out
10	60
20	70
30	80
40	90

2. Counting by tens in both columns; adding 50 in each row

Week 2: Day 4 (page 21)

1. Possible answer: Student 2 completed the table correctly because 8 + 12 = 20.
2. Possible answer: The sums all equal 20. The first addend increases by 1 until the last row. The second addend decreases by 1 until the last row. These patterns make sense because when the first addend increases by one then the second addend must decrease by one so that the sum is still 20.

Week 2: Day 5 (page 22)

1. Possible strategies: drawing a picture, making a table, using a number line
2. 36 stickers; Possible answer: I drew a picture to show how many stickers are in each row. Then, I counted all of the stickers.

Week 3: Day 1 (page 23)

1. Possible answer: I would line up the numbers vertically by place value and add them.
2. Possible answer: Since the first number is 5,000, I know I should put a 5 in the thousands place. The 900 shows I should put a 9 in the hundreds place. Then, I will put a 3 in the tens place and a 2 in the ones place.

Week 3: Day 2 (page 24)

1. 5,932; answer has 4 digits and goes to the thousands place value; put each digit in its correct place value
2. 2,711; answer has 4 digits and goes to the thousands place value; put each digit in its correct place

ANSWER KEY (cont.)

Week 3: Day 3 (page 25)

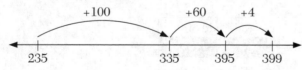

235 + 100 + 60 + 4 = 399; 235 + 164 = 399

Week 3: Day 4 (page 26)
1. Possible answers: pictures, base-10 blocks, place value chart, equations; 355 + 150 = 505; 505 − 275 = 230
2. Possible answer: I think it's better to add the left side of the equation. Then, subtract 275 from the sum.

Week 3: Day 5 (page 27)
1. 866 baked items; Possible strategies: pictures, base-10 blocks, place value chart, equations; 167 + 233 + 329 + 137 = 866
2. Tuesday; Possible answer: I added the total number of baked items they sold on each day. Then, I compared the totals.

Week 4: Day 1 (page 28)
1. Possible answer: Each number in the subtraction problem has one more zero than the one before it. The numbers increase from ones, to tens, to hundreds, to thousands.
2. The pattern does not work because the numbers do not have the same number of zeroes. One number goes to the hundreds place and the other only goes to the tens place.

Week 4: Day 2 (page 29)
1. 4; 40; 400; 4,000; basic fact 9 − 5 = 4 is the same in each equation; use this basic fact to solve and look for patterns with zeroes
2. 7; 150; 700; 8,000; basic fact 15 − 8 = 7 is the same in each equation; need to find the missing number in the fact and look for patterns with zeroes

Week 4: Day 3 (page 30)
1. 21 + 200 + 62 = 283; 562 − 279 = 283

Week 4: Day 4 (page 31)
1. 411; Possible strategies: regrouping, counting up, number line, base-10 blocks, pictures, equation; 740 − 329 = 411
2. Possible answer: I like subtracting with regrouping because I can regroup 1 ten into 10 ones, then subtract in the ones place.

Week 4: Day 5 (page 32)
1. 222 pages; Possible strategies: add the total number of pages (26 + 57 = 83), then subtract the sum from 305 (305 − 83 = 222); subtract 26 from 305 (305 − 26 = 279), then subtract 57 from the difference (279 − 57 = 222)
2. Possible answer: I can add my answer (222) to the total number of pages he read (83) to see if it gives me 305 (222 + 83 = 305).

Week 5: Day 1 (page 33)
1. Shawn has 65 crayons. He has 38 left after giving some to his sister.
2. Possible question: How many crayons did Shawn give to his sister?

Week 5: Day 2 (page 34)
1. 27 crayons; write a subtraction equation to find how much he has left; 65 − c = 38
2. 76 comic books; write a subtraction equation to find how many he started with; b − 14 = 62

Week 5: Day 3 (page 35)
600, 400, 200; total = 1,200

Week 5: Day 4 (page 36)
1. 24 people; Possible strategies: pictures, base-10 blocks, write equations: 32 − 12 − 6 + 10 = 24; 32 − (12 + 6) + 10 = 24; 32 − 12 = 20 − 6 = 14 + 10 = 24
2. Possible answer: I like the picture strategy because it is easy for me to see the people getting on and getting off the bus.

Week 5: Day 5 (page 37)
1. 240 notes; Possible answer: I know that Dr. Callahan will write 60 notes each week. After 4 weeks, she will write 240 notes. I added 4 groups of 60 to find the solution.
2. 120 students; 60 + 60 + 60 + 60 = 240; 360 − 240 = 120

Week 6: Day 1 (page 38)
1. To find a product, find the first factor on the left and the second factor at the top (or the other way around). Where they meet in the chart is their product.
2. Possible answer: The numbers in the "2" column are counting by 2s.

ANSWER KEY *(cont.)*

Week 6: Day 2 (page 39)

1. Find missing multiplication facts; use skip-counting patterns

×	1	2	3	4
1	1	2	3	4
2	2	4	6	8
3	3	6	9	12
4	4	8	12	16

2. Find missing multiplication facts; use skip-counting patterns

×	5	6	7	8
2	10	12	14	16
3	15	18	21	24
4	20	24	28	32
5	25	30	35	40

Week 6: Day 3 (page 40)

1.

Rule: × 5	
In	Out
1	5
2	10
3	15
4	20

2. Counting by ones in first column; counting by fives in second column; multiplying by 5 in each row

Week 6: Day 4 (page 41)

1. Jasmine does not have enough cards. She has 32 cards, but needs 40 cards. 4 × 8 = 32; 32 < 40; Possible strategies: picture, array model, tally marks, number line, skip-counting pattern

2. Possible answer: I think drawing an array is the best strategy because I can put the cards in 4 rows with 8 cards in each row and then count them up.

Week 6: Day 5 (page 42)

1. 9 flowers; 3 × 3 = 9
2. 54 seeds; 6 × 9 = 54

Week 7: Day 1 (page 43)

1. Repeated addition is a strategy that can be used when adding the same number over and over again.

2. Multiplication is a strategy that can be used when each group has the same number of objects.

Week 7: Day 2 (page 44)

1. 4 + 4 + 4 = 12, 3 × 4 = 12; there are 3 bags and each one has 4 apples inside; use repeated addition, then write a multiplication equation

2. 5 + 5 + 5 + 5 = 20, 4 × 5 = 20; there are 4 bags and each one has 5 peaches inside; use repeated addition, then write a multiplication equation

Week 7: Day 3 (page 45)

7 × 3 = 21

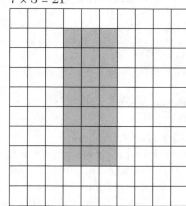

Week 7: Day 4 (page 46)

1. 6 × 3 = 18; Possible strategies: array model, equal groups model; picture, repeated addition

2. Possible answer: I like using a number line because it helps me see the pattern when skip counting.

Week 7: Day 5 (page 47)

1. Drawings of arrays should include: 2 × 12 = 24 and 12 × 2 = 24; 3 × 8 = 24 and 8 × 3 = 24; 4 × 6 = 24 and 6 × 4 = 24

2. 6; Possible answer: The arrays with the same factors have the same product.

ANSWER KEY *(cont.)*

Week 8: Day 1 (page 48)

1. Possible strategies: array model, equal groups model; picture, repeated addition
2. Possible answer: I will write the products less than 20 in the first column, the products equal to 20 in the middle column, and the products greater than 20 in the last column.

Week 8: Day 2 (page 49)

1. Find the products for each equation; write the equations in the correct place in the table

Product < 20	Product = 20	Product > 20
3 × 6 =18	4 × 5 = 20 2 × 10 = 20	5 × 5 = 25

2. Find the products for each equation; write the equations in the correct place in the table

Product < 40	Product = 40	Product > 40
9 × 4 = 36	8 × 5 = 40 4 × 10 = 40	6 × 7 = 42

Week 8: Day 3 (page 50)

1. 8 breaks apart into 5 + 3; 5 × 6 = 30; 3 × 6 = 18; 30 + 18 = 48
2. 6 breaks apart into 3 + 3; 3 × 9 = 27; 3 × 9 = 27; 27 + 27 = 54

Week 8: Day 4 (page 51)

1. 8 × 9 = 72 flyers; Possible strategies: picture, repeated addition, equal groups model, array model, break apart a factor into 2 addends
2. Possible answer: I prefer to break apart one of the factors because I don't know my 8 facts yet, but I do know my 5 facts and 3 facts.

Week 8: Day 5 (page 52)

1. 1 × 36 = 36, 36 × 1 = 36, 2 × 18 = 36, 18 × 2 = 36, 3 × 12 = 36, 12 × 3 = 36, 4 × 9 = 36, 9 × 4 = 36, 6 × 6 = 36
2. 9
3. Yes, some equations have the same factors, but they are just switched.

Week 9: Day 1 (page 53)

1. The number line is counting by 60s. The numbers on the number line are increasing by 60 each time.
2. Skip count on the number line 4 times starting at 0

Week 9: Day 2 (page 54)

1. 240; number line is counting by 60s; make 4 hops from 0; 4 × 60 = 240
2. 150; multiplying by 50; number line should count by 50s; fill in the missing parts of the number line; 3 × 50 = 150; Missing numbers on the number line should be 100 and 150

Week 9: Day 3 (page 55)

6 groups of 3 tens = 18 tens; 6 × 30 = 180

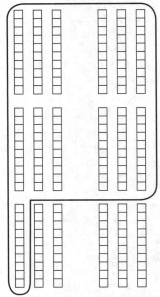

Week 9: Day 4 (page 56)

1. 6 × 70 = 420; Possible strategies: base-10 blocks, number line, picture, equal-groups model, repeated addition
2. Possible answer: I think using repeated addition is easier because I can add 6 groups of 70. For example, 70 + 70 + 70 + 70 + 70 + 70 = 420.

Week 9: Day 5 (page 57)

1. Possible models: base-10 blocks, number line, picture, equal-groups model
2. 250 markers; Possible answer: I found 5 groups of 20, which is 100. Then, I found 5 groups of 30, which is 150. I added 100 and 150 to find the total, which is 250.

Week 10: Day 1 (page 58)

1. There are 8 goldfish and 4 bowls. Each bowl has the same number of fish.
2. Write a division equation to find how many fish are in each bowl.

ANSWER KEY (cont.)

Week 10: Day 2 (page 59)

1. 2 fish in each bowl; $8 \div 4 = 2$; there are 8 goldfish total, divided into 4 equal groups; draw a picture of 4 bowls and put a fish in each bowl until I count to 8
2. 6 turtles in each tank; $18 \div 3 = 6$; there are 18 turtles total, divided into 3 equal groups; draw a picture of 3 tanks and put a turtle in each tank until I count to 18

Week 10: Day 3 (page 60)

1.

Total	Number of equal groups	Number in each group	Division fact
56	8	7	$56 \div 8 = 7$
50	10	5	$50 \div 10 = 5$
28	4	7	$28 \div 4 = 7$
64	8	8	$64 \div 8 = 8$

2.

Total	Number of equal groups	Number in each group	Division fact
12	2	6	$12 \div 2 = 6$
20	4	5	$20 \div 4 = 5$
18	6	3	$18 \div 6 = 3$
72	8	9	$72 \div 8 = 9$

Week 10: Day 4 (page 61)

1. 8 cards; $72 \div 9 = 8$; Possible strategies: picture, repeated subtraction, number line, multiplication fact
2. Possible answer: I think drawing 9 circles and counting out 72 tallies equally is easiest because it doesn't take much time and I can get the right answer even if I cannot remember the fact.

Week 10: Day 5 (page 62)

1. Drawings should show 4 trophies on each of the 3 shelves with 1 trophy left over.
2. Possible answer: I can change the 13 to 12, because 12 can be divided by 3 evenly and there is nothing left over.

Week 11: Day 1 (page 63)

1. The division fact is given. The number 63 is divided into an unknown number of bags. There are 9 seashells in each bag.
2. Possible answer: I would turn the division equation into a multiplication fact and think, what number times 9 equals 63?

Week 11: Day 2 (page 64)

7 bags; $63 \div 7 = 9$; a division fact is given; use multiplication facts to find the missing number of the division fact; make an equals-groups model

Week 11: Day 3 (page 65)

$20 \div 4 = 5$; 4 rows

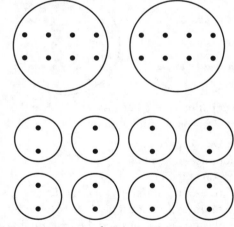

Week 11: Day 4 (page 66)

1. 8 days; Possible strategies: picture, repeated subtraction, array model, equal-groups model, multiplication equation, division equation
2. Possible answer: I like drawing a picture because it helps me see the problem.

Week 11: Day 5 (page 67)

1. Possible pictures:

2. James is correct because $16 \div 8 = 2$.
3. Matt is wrong because $4 \div 8 = 2$ is not correct.

Week 12: Day 1 (page 68)

1. The number 9 is on both sides of the equation. The number 3 is on one side, but there is a missing number on the other side of the equation. Factors in a multiplication equation can be in any order and still give the same product.
2. Possible answer: I will look on the left side of the equal sign to see what factor is missing on the right side of the equal sign.

ANSWER KEY *(cont.)*

Week 12: Day 2 (page 69)
1. $9 \times 3 = 3 \times 9$; draw a picture of 9 groups of 3 to find the product, then find how many groups of 9 will give the same product
2. $6 \times 7 = 7 \times 6$; draw an array with 6 rows of 7 to find the product, then find how many rows of 6 will give the same product

Week 12: Day 3 (page 70)
$6 \times 7 = (6 \times 4) + (6 \times 3)$
$6 \times 7 = 24 + 18$
$6 \times 7 = 42$

Week 12: Day 4 (page 71)
1. 60 model cars; $4 \times 5 \times 3 = 60$; Possible strategies: picture, array model, equal-groups model, multiplication equation
2. Possible answer: I like to draw a picture because I can use arrays to show the problem.

Week 12: Day 5 (page 72)
1. Possible picture:

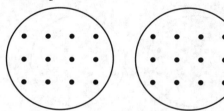

2. The equation is true because $4 \times 2 = 8$ and $8 \times 3 = 24$. Both problems equal 24.

Week 13: Day 1 (page 73)
1. 2 multiplication equations
2. 2 division equations
3. The order of the numbers matters. The largest number, 28, must be the answer in the multiplication equations and the first number (dividend) in the division equations.

Week 13: Day 2 (page 74)
1. $7 \times 4 = 28$, $4 \times 7 = 28$, $28 \div 7 = 4$, $28 \div 4 = 7$; write 2 multiplication equations and 2 division equations; put the largest number, 28, as the answer for the multiplication equations and as the first number in the division equations
2. $6 \times 9 = 54$, $9 \times 6 = 54$, $54 \div 6 = 9$, $54 \div 9 = 6$; write 2 multiplication equations and 2 division equations; put the largest number, 54, as the answer for the multiplication equations and as the first number in the division equations

Week 13: Day 3 (page 75)
$4 \times 9 = 36$; $9 \times 4 = 36$; $36 \div 4 = 9$; $36 \div 9 = 4$

Week 13: Day 4 (page 76)
1. 8 friends; $4 \times 8 = 32$, $8 \times 4 = 32$, $32 \div 4 = 8$, $32 \div 8 = 4$; Possible strategies: array model, equal-groups model, picture, fact families, bar model
2. Possible answer: I think drawing an array is better because it helps me to organize my work and find the answer.

Week 13: Day 5 (page 77)
1. $3 \times 8 = 24$; $8 \times 3 = 24$; $24 \div 3 = 8$; $24 \div 8 = 3$;
$4 \times 6 = 24$; $6 \times 4 = 24$; $24 \div 4 = 6$; $24 \div 6 = 4$;
$24 \times 1 = 24$; $1 \times 24 = 24$; $24 \div 1 = 24$; $24 \div 24 = 1$;
$2 \times 12 = 24$; $12 \times 2 = 24$; $24 \div 2 = 12$; $24 \div 12 = 2$
2. Possible picture:

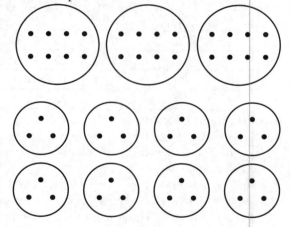

Week 14: Day 1 (page 78)
1. Four numbers are given and a blank division equation with the quotient 3.
2. Possible answer: A strategy I would use is to try different combinations of the given numbers until I find two that, when divided, will give the quotient 3.

ANSWER KEY *(cont.)*

Week 14: Day 2 (page 79)
1. $21 \div 7 = 3$; find two numbers that when divided give the quotient 3; draw a picture to find the missing numbers in the division equation
2. $40 \div 5 = 8$; find two numbers that when divided give the quotient 8; use known multiplication facts to find the missing numbers in the division equation

Week 14: Day 3 (page 80)

Double (× 2)	Double Double (× 4)	Double Double Double (× 8)
$2 \times 6 = ?$ Since, $2 \times 6 = 12$, then $12 \div 2 = 6$ and $12 \div 6 = 2$.	$4 \times 8 = ?$ $2 \times 8 = 16$ $2 \times 16 = 32$ Since, $4 \times 8 = 32$, then $32 \div 4 = 8$ and $32 \div 8 = 4$.	$8 \times 6 = ?$ $2 \times 6 = 12$ $2 \times 12 = 24$ $2 \times 24 = 48$ Since, $8 \times 6 = 48$, then $48 \div 8 = 6$ and $48 \div 6 = 8$.

Week 14: Day 4 (page 81)
1. Possible strategies: array model, equal-groups model, picture, bar model

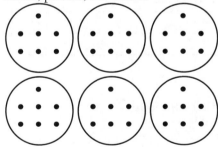

2. Possible answer: I think drawing an equal-groups model is easier because it helps me find how many are in each group.

Week 14: Day 5 (page 82)
1. 54 pictures; $9 \times 6 = 54$; Possible picture:

2. Yes, there will be 4 pictures left over. There are a total of 54 pictures. The scrapbook only holds 50 pictures, so there are 4 left over.

Week 15: Day 1 (page 83)
1. There are 5 groups with 6 students in each group.
2. Possible answer: I will think of the facts $5 \times 6 = ?$, $6 \times 5 = ?$, $? \div 5 = 6$, and $? \div 6 = 5$.

Week 15: Day 2 (page 84)
1. 30 students; use fact families; $5 \times 6 = 30$, $6 \times 5 = 30$, $30 \div 5 = 6$, and $30 \div 6 = 5$.
2. 7 students; use fact families; $9 \times 7 = 63$, $7 \times 9 = 63$, $63 \div 9 = 7$, and $63 \div 7 = 9$.

Week 15: Day 3 (page 85)
$4 \times 7 = 28$; Students should have drawn 7 cookies in each bag.

Week 15: Day 4 (page 86)
1. 8 tokens; $40 \div 5 = 8$; Possible strategies: bar model, fact families, picture, array model, equal-groups model
2. Possible answer: I like using a fact family because I am faster at doing multiplication than division.

Week 15: Day 5 (page 87)
1. 36 pieces of pie; $6 \times 6 = 36$; Possible picture:

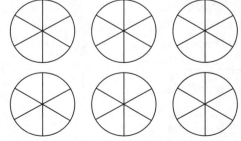

2. 4 pieces of pie; Possible answer: There are 36 pieces total. Since 9 people will share them, each person will get 4 pieces of pie.

ANSWER KEY *(cont.)*

Week 16: Day 1 (page 88)
1. Nick spent $5 buying supplies. He charged $2 per glass and earned $15 total.
2. The letter *g* stands for the total number of glasses he sold.

Week 16: Day 2 (page 89)
1. B. $2 \times g - 5 = 15$; reread the question and look at each answer choice to see if the given information and letter *g* in each equation makes sense for the problem
2. A. $(4 \times 10) + (5 \times c) = 60$; reread the question and look at each answer choice to see if the given information and letter *c* in each equation makes sense for the problem

Week 16: Day 3 (page 90)
$14 - 5 = 9$; $14 + 9 = 23$ pencils

Week 16: Day 4 (page 91)
1. $10; $30 - 13 = 17$, $17 - 7 = 10$; Possible strategies: picture, bar model, equations
2. Possible answer: I think writing equations is easier because I can use place value to find my answer faster.

Week 16: Day 5 (page 92)
1. $182; $7 \times 10 = 70$, $70 + 112 = 182$
2. No; Emily has $182. The bike costs $225. Emily needs an additional $43 to buy the bike.

Week 17: Day 1 (page 93)
1. Hector cut a sandwich in halves.
2. Halves means to divide something into 2 equal parts.

Week 17: Day 2 (page 94)
1. 2 equal parts; draw a square divided into 2 equal parts
2. 3 equal parts; draw a rectangle divided into 3 equal parts

Week 17: Day 3 (page 95)
$\frac{1}{6}$; Possible model:

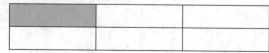

Week 17: Day 4 (page 96)
1. $\frac{1}{4}$; Possible strategies: picture, fraction bars; unit fractions
2. Possible answer: I like using fraction bars because it helps me understand how to partition a shape into equal parts.

Week 17: Day 5 (page 97)
1. Possible model:

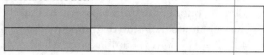

2. Yes, Destiny is correct. Since her family ate 3 of the 6 pieces, they ate $\frac{1}{2}$ of the cake.

Week 18: Day 1 (page 98)
1. 4 equal parts
2. The numerator tells you how many parts of the whole you are counting.

Week 18: Day 2 (page 99)
1. The number line is divided into 4 equal parts; label each fraction on the number line

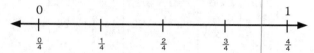

2. The number line is divided into 6 equal parts; label each fraction on the number line

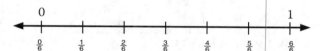

Week 18: Day 3 (page 100)

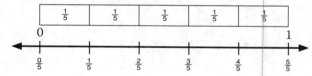

Week 18: Day 4 (page 101)
1. $\frac{1}{7}$; Possible strategies: picture, number line
2. Possible answer: I like drawing a picture because it helps me visualize what is happening in the problem.

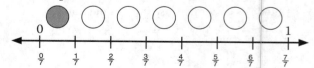

ANSWER KEY (cont.)

Week 18: Day 5 (page 102)
1. $\frac{1}{4}$
2. $\frac{1}{2}$
3. Possible explanation: I put $\frac{1}{2}$ in the middle of 0 and 1. Then, I thought about dividing the number line into fourths and found $\frac{1}{4}$. Lastly, I know that $\frac{1}{3}$ is greater than $\frac{1}{4}$, but less than $\frac{1}{2}$, so I put $\frac{1}{3}$ between $\frac{1}{4}$ and $\frac{1}{2}$.

Week 19: Day 1 (page 103)
1. 4 equal parts; Possible answer: the number line shows 4 equal parts between 0 and 1.
2. To find the numerators for the missing fractions, think about what number comes after 1 and what number comes after 3 on the number line.

Week 19: Day 2 (page 104)
1. $\frac{2}{4}$; $\frac{4}{4}$; number line is divided into fourths; write 4 as the denominator, count to find the numerators for the missing fractions
2. $\frac{2}{6}$; $\frac{4}{6}$; $\frac{6}{6}$; number line is divided into sixths; write 6 as the denominator, count to find the numerators for the missing fractions

Week 19: Day 3 (page 105)

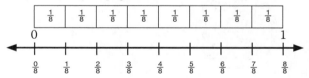

Week 19: Day 4 (page 106)
1. Possible strategies: fraction model, number line; fraction model should have 3 parts out of 6 parts shaded

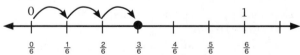

2. Possible answer: I like to draw a circle and divide it into sixths because it helps me see the problem.

Week 19: Day 5 (page 107)
1. $\frac{4}{3}$ miles; Missing fractions: $\frac{2}{3}$, $\frac{4}{3}$, $\frac{6}{3}$; Possible explanation: I used the number line to skip count by $\frac{1}{3}$. I made two hops for $\frac{2}{3}$ and two more hops for another $\frac{2}{3}$. I landed on $\frac{4}{3}$.

2. The bus traveled more than 1 mile. Since $\frac{3}{3}$ is equal to 1, then $\frac{4}{3}$ is greater than $\frac{3}{3}$ or 1.

Week 20: Day 1 (page 108)
1. Equivalent fractions are fractions that are equal to each other even though they have different numerators and denominators.
2. Both circles are the same size and have the same amount shaded.
3. The circles are different because the first is divided into halves and the second is divided into fourths.

Week 20: Day 2 (page 109)
1. $\frac{1}{2} = \frac{2}{4}$; first circle is divided into halves and second is divided in fourths; count how many fourths are shaded to equal $\frac{1}{2}$
2. $\frac{2}{3} = \frac{4}{6}$; first rectangle is divided into thirds and the second is divided into sixths; count how many sixths are shaded to equal $\frac{2}{3}$

Week 20: Day 3 (page 110)
$\frac{1}{2} = \frac{3}{6}$

Week 20: Day 4 (page 111)
1. $\frac{5}{10}$ is less; Possible strategies: fraction model, number line

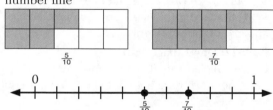

2. Possible answer: I like drawing a fraction model because I think it's easier to make tenths on a rectangle than on a number line.

Week 20: Day 5 (page 112)
1. Order of fractions on the number line: $\frac{1}{7}$, $\frac{3}{7}$, $\frac{4}{7}$, $\frac{7}{7}$; Possible explanation: Since the denominator of each fraction is 7, I drew tick marks on the number line by dividing it into 7 equal parts. I looked at the numerators to order the fractions from least to greatest.
2. The fraction $\frac{7}{7}$ is the greatest because it is equal to 1. The other fractions are less than 1.

Week 21: Day 1 (page 113)
1. Kevin ate $\frac{1}{4}$ of his pizza and Monique ate $\frac{2}{8}$ of her pizza.
2. Possible answer: I will shade the amount of pizza each person ate and compare them.

ANSWER KEY *(cont.)*

Week 21: Day 2 (page 114)
1. Yes; $\frac{1}{4}$ is equal to $\frac{2}{8}$; shade in the amount of pizza each person ate and compare them
2. No; $\frac{2}{3}$ is not equal to $\frac{5}{6}$; shade in the amount of the fruit bar each person ate and compare them

Week 21: Day 3 (page 115)
$\frac{1}{3}, \frac{5}{8}, \frac{3}{4}$

Week 21: Day 4 (page 116)
1. $\frac{1}{2} = \frac{3}{6}$; Possible strategies: fraction model, number line
2. Possible answer: I think drawing a fraction model is easier because it helps me to compare fractions to see if the amounts are equal.

Week 21: Day 5 (page 117)
1. Possible model:

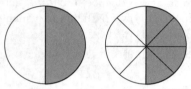

2. Possible answer: I disagree with Max. Joey and Max ate the same amount because $\frac{1}{2} = \frac{4}{8}$.
3. $\frac{4}{8}$; Since Max ate $\frac{4}{8}$, or $\frac{1}{2}$, of the pizza, he has $\frac{4}{8}$, or $\frac{1}{2}$, of the pizza left.

Week 22: Day 1 (page 118)
1. Possible answer: The numerator and denominator are both 5. I know that $\frac{5}{5}$ is equal to 1.
2. $\frac{1}{5}$; Possible answer: Each part of the number line is $\frac{1}{5}$ of the whole.

Week 22: Day 2 (page 119)
1. Divide the number line into fifths; place a point on $\frac{5}{5}$, or 1.

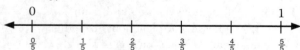

2. Divide the number line into tenths; place a point on $\frac{10}{10}$, or 1.

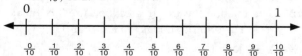

Week 22: Day 3 (page 120)

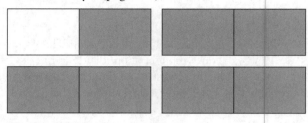

Week 22: Day 4 (page 121)
1. $\frac{11}{6}$; Model should show 1 part shaded; Possible strategies: fraction model, number line
2. Possible answer: I think drawing a picture of the muffin trays divided into 6 parts is easier because it helps me see the problem.

Week 22: Day 5 (page 122)
1. Possible model:

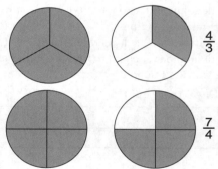

2. $\frac{7}{4}$ pounds; Possible explanation: I know that the apple that is $\frac{7}{4}$ pounds weighs more because my model for $\frac{7}{4}$ has more shaded.

Week 23: Day 1 (page 123)
1. Count the equal parts on the number line between 0 and 1.
2. Fractions that are closer to 1 are greater than fractions closer to 0.

ANSWER KEY *(cont.)*

Week 23: Day 2 (page 124)
1. Number line shows fifths; label the fractions on the number line; circle the fraction closer to 1.

2. Number line shows fourths; label the fractions on the number line; circle the fraction closer to 0.

Week 23: Day 3 (page 125)
$\frac{2}{3} = \frac{4}{6}$; Possible picture:

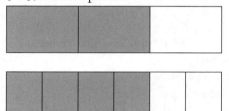

Week 23: Day 4 (page 126)
1. Alejandro; Possible strategies: fraction model, number line, picture
2. Possible answer: I think drawing a picture is easier because it looks like a sandwich and helps me visualize the problem better.

Week 23: Day 5 (page 127)
1. Possible model:

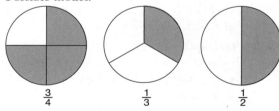

2. $\frac{1}{3}$, $\frac{1}{2}$, $\frac{3}{4}$; Possible answer: I drew a model for each fraction and compared the parts shaded to order them from least to greatest.

Week 24: Day 1 (page 128)
1. 60 minutes; Possible answer: Using a clock, I can count by fives from 12 until I get back to 12.
2. Possible answer: I can count by fives until I get to 20, then I can count by ones.

Week 24: Day 2 (page 129)
23 minutes; count by fives starting from 0 to 20, then count 3 more

Week 24: Day 3 (page 130)
3:38

Week 24: Day 4 (page 131)
1. Possible strategies: number line, clock; number line and clock should show the time 4:26
2. Possible answer: I like using a clock better because the hands on the clock help me to read the time.

Week 24: Day 5 (page 132)
1. 27 minutes; Possible model:

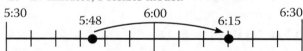

2. Less than $\frac{1}{2}$ hour; Possible explanation: My answer is 27 minutes, which is less than $\frac{1}{2}$ hour, or 30 minutes.

Week 25: Day 1 (page 133)
1. The first number shows the hour.
2. The second number shows the minutes.
3. Possible question: What time will Linda get home from school?

Week 25: Day 2 (page 134)
1. 1:43; add 20 minutes to 1:23; the hour will stay the same since the minutes are less than 60
2. 2:34; add 15 minutes to 2:19; the hour will stay the same since the minutes are less than 60

Week 25: Day 3 (page 135)
6:15

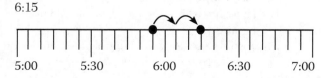

ANSWER KEY *(cont.)*

Week 25: Day 4 (page 136)
1. 75 minutes or 1 hour 15 minutes; Possible strategies: number line, picture, clock
2. Possible answer: I like to use a number line because I can count by fives to find the number of minutes.

Week 25: Day 5 (page 137)
1. Reading is 1 hour and 15 minutes, writing is 45 minutes, reading is 30 minutes longer; Possible models: number line, clock, picture
2. 2 hours and 45 minutes; Possible explanation: I found the time by counting 2 hours from 8:15 to 10:15, then adding 45 minutes to get to 11:00.

Week 26: Day 1 (page 138)
1. grams
2. kilograms
3. paperclip, pencil
4. book, desk

Week 26: Day 2 (page 139)
1. grams: paperclip, pencil; kilograms: book, desk; think about how much each item weighs; decide if using grams or kilograms is better
2. milliliters: juice box, cup of milk; liters: pitcher of water, pot of soup; think about how much each item weighs; decide if using milliliters or liters is better

Week 26: Day 3 (page 140)
glass of lemonade: about 1 liter; bottle of water: about 1 liter; spoonful of medicine: about 1 milliliter

Week 26: Day 4 (page 141)
1. Possible strategies: using a balance, comparing weights by holding the textbook in one hand and the laptop in the other hand
2. Possible answer: I think comparing weights by holding the objects is better because you may not have a balance to use.

Week 26: Day 5 (page 142)
1. Possible models: fraction model, picture, number line
2. Yes, the four glasses together hold 6 liters because 4 groups of $1\frac{1}{2}$ is 6.

Week 27: Day 1 (page 143)
1. There are 9 cherries and each one weighs 4 grams.
2. Possible answer: I will multiply the number of cherries by the weight of each cherry.

Week 27: Day 2 (page 144)
1. 36 grams; 9 × 4 = 36; multiply the number of cherries (9) by the weight of each cherry (4 grams); solve using repeated addition
2. 7 grams; 63 ÷ 9 = 7; divide the weight of the strawberries (63 grams) by the number of strawberries in the basket (9); solve by repeated subtraction

Week 27: Day 3 (page 145)
480 milliliters of water: 160 + 320 = 480

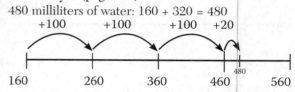

Week 27: Day 4 (page 146)
1. 29 liters; 56 − 27 = 29; Possible strategies: number line, picture, subtraction equation
2. Possible answer: I think using a subtraction equation is easier because it is faster and easier than drawing a picture.

Week 27: Day 5 (page 147)
1. 45 grams; Possible strategies: picture, addition and multiplication equations
2. Possible explanation: I found the total mass by adding the mass of each item. I used multiplication for the equal groups that repeated to find my answer faster.

Week 28: Day 1 (page 148)
1. 2 books
2. Possible questions: How many books does Ty read in October? How many more books did Ty read in November than September?

Week 28: Day 2 (page 149)
6 books; 2 × 3 = 6; each picture stands for 2 books; there are 3 books for October; solve 2 × 3 to get the answer

ANSWER KEY *(cont.)*

Week 28: Day 3 (page 150)

Favorite Type of Cookie		
chocolate chip	卌 卌 卌 I	● ● ● ●
peanut butter	卌 卌	● ● ◗
oatmeal raisin	卌 I	● ◗
sugar cookie	卌 卌 卌 卌	● ● ● ● ● ●
Key: Each ● = 4 votes		

Week 28: Day 4 (page 151)

1. 45 students; Possible strategies: add votes for zoo and park, add votes for art and history museum, then subtract; add zoo and park pictures, add art and history museum pictures, subtract, then multiply by 10
2. Possible answer: I think adding the zoo and park votes, then adding the art and history museum votes, and then subtracting these answers is easiest. I am better at adding and subtracting than multiplying.

Week 28: Day 5 (page 152)

1. 40 goals; 6 + 3 + 10 + 9 + 7 + 5 = 40; Possible picture graph:

Title: Lightning Soccer Goals	
Lucy	⚽ ⚽ ⚽ ⚽ ⚽ ⚽
Marco	⚽ ⚽ ⚽
Charlie	⚽ ⚽ ⚽ ⚽ ⚽ ⚽ ⚽ ⚽ ⚽ ⚽
David	⚽ ⚽ ⚽ ⚽ ⚽ ⚽ ⚽ ⚽ ⚽
Julie	⚽ ⚽ ⚽ ⚽ ⚽ ⚽ ⚽
Grace	⚽ ⚽ ⚽ ⚽ ⚽
Key: Each ⚽ = 1 goal	

2. 4 goals; Possible explanation: I added the number of goals for the boys. Then, added the number of goals for the girls. Lastly, I subtracted the sums to find the answer.

Week 29: Day 1 (page 153)

1. The graph shows how many pictures Perry took during the four days of his vacation.
2. Fewest means the smallest number.

Week 29: Day 2 (page 154)

Wednesday; look at the height of each bar and compare them; find the shortest bar

Week 29: Day 3 (page 155)

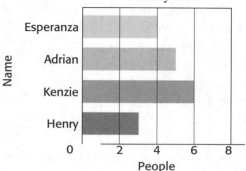

Family Size

Week 29: Day 4 (page 156)

1. 6 miles; 7 + 3 + 4 + 5 + 3 + 2 = 24, 30 − 24 = 6; Possible strategies: adding up the bars and subtracting from 30; subtracting each individual bar from 30; pictures, tallies
2. Possible answer: I think adding up all of the miles and subtracting that number from 30 is better because I can add numbers much faster than subtracting them.

Week 29: Day 5 (page 157)

1. 22 students; 4 + 3 + 1 + 8 + 6 = 22

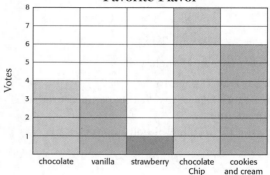

Favorite Flavor

ANSWER KEY *(cont.)*

2. Possible question: How many more students voted for chocolate and chocolate chip than strawberry and cookies and cream?; 5 students; $12 - 7 = 5$

Week 30: Day 1 (page 158)
1. Number of inches
2. The inch that the line is closest to

Week 30: Day 2 (page 159)
1. 3 inches; measure the line to the nearest inch; compare the length of crayon line to the ruler and see which inch it is closest to
2. $1\frac{1}{2}$ inches; measure the line to the nearest half inch; compare the length of the paper clip to the ruler and see which inch or $\frac{1}{2}$ inch it is closest to

Week 30: Day 3 (page 160)

Shoelance Lengths

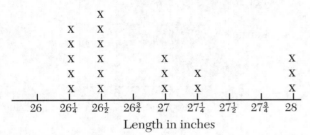

Length in inches

Week 30: Day 4 (page 161)
1. Student 2: Possible strategies: ruler; look to see who lined up the pencil correctly with the ruler
2. Possible answer: Student 1 lined up the pencil with 1 instead of 0.

Week 30: Day 5 (page 162)
1.

String Length

		X	X	
	X	X	X	X
2	$2\frac{1}{2}$	3	$3\frac{1}{2}$	4

Length in inches

2. Between 2 and 3 inches

Week 31: Day 1 (page 163)
1. Amount of space inside a shape; measured in square units
2. Count the number of unit squares

Week 31: Day 2 (page 164)
1. 8 square units; each square is one square unit; count the squares in the shape
2. 9 square units; each square is one square unit; count the squares in the shape

Week 31: Day 3 (page 165)
Possible dimensions of shapes: 2 by 6, 6 by 2, 12 by 1, 1 by 12, 3 by 4, 4 by 3

Week 31: Day 4 (page 166)
1. Possible dimensions of shapes: 3 by 8, 8 by 3, 4 by 6, 6 by 4
2. Possible answer: I think a 4 by 6 or 6 by 4 space is better because it gives the dog a wider space to play.

Week 31: Day 5 (page 167)
1. Yes; possible answer: The area of all the furniture is less than the area of the bedroom.

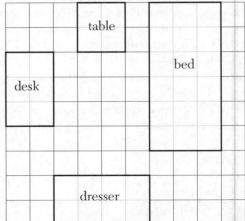

2. 36 square units; Possible answer: I added the number of square units for each piece of furniture to find the total number of square units.

Week 32: Day 1 (page 168)
1. Count the number of unit squares
2. Square inches

Week 32: Day 2 (page 169)
1. 16 square inches; each unit square is 1 square inch; count the number of unit squares
2. 14 square feet; each unit square is 1 square foot; count the number of unit squares

Week 32: Day 3 (page 170)
Possible dimensions of shapes: 2 by 8, 8 by 2, 4 by 4

ANSWER KEY *(cont.)*

Week 32: Day 4 (page 171)
1. Possible dimensions of shapes: 4 by 9, 9 by 4, 6 by 6
2. Possible answer: I think a 6 by 6 space is better because it is a wider space for a bathroom.

Week 32: Day 5 (page 172)
Students should have 5 or more shapes drawn on the graph paper; Total number of square feet and explanations will vary, but students' explanations should represent their drawings.

Week 33: Day 1 (page 173)
1. Drawing of rectangle with unit squares; dimensions of rectangle
2. Multiply the length by the width; multiply the width by the length

Week 33: Day 2 (page 174)
1. 18 square units; $3 \times 6 = 18$; rectangle is 3 units by 6 units; multiply the length and the width
2. 16 square units; $2 \times 8 = 16$; rectangle is 2 units by 8 units; multiply the length and the width

Week 33: Day 3 (page 175)
15 square feet; $5 \times 3 = 15$

Week 33: Day 4 (page 176)
1. 8 feet; Possible strategies: picture, division equation; fact families; repeated subtraction, array model, equal-groups model
2. Possible answer: I think writing a division equation is easier because it is faster than drawing a picture.

Week 33: Day 5 (page 177)
1. Drawings should show a rectangle that is 9 meters long and 7 meters wide.
2. 7 bags of grass seed; Possible explanation: The area of the space is 63 square meters. Since 1 bag of grass seed covers 10 square meters, he will need more than 6 bags, but less than 7 bags.

Week 34: Day 1 (page 178)
1. Perimeter measures the distance around a shape and area measures the space inside the shape.
2. Add the length of each of the four sides

Week 34: Day 2 (page 179)
1. 26 inches; $8 + 8 + 5 + 5 = 26$; perimeter is the distance around the desk; add all of the lengths together
2. 28 feet of fencing; $4 + 4 + 3 + 3 + 7 + 7 = 28$; perimeter is the distance around the garden; add all of the lengths together

Week 34: Day 3 (page 180)
$5 + 3 + 2 + 11 + 7 = 28$; $36 - 28 = 8$; $j = 8$ inches

Week 34: Day 4 (page 181)
1. Yes, perimeter of the bulletin board is 24 feet and she has 30 feet of border; $8 + 8 + 4 + 4 = 24$ or $(8 \times 2) + (4 \times 2) = 24$; $30 - 24 = 6$; Possible strategies: picture, area model, addition, multiplication, subtraction
2. Possible answer: I think drawing a picture is easier because it helps me visualize the problem.

Week 34: Day 5 (page 182)
1. 2 square centimeters by 8 square centimeters; Possible explanation: I found the perimeter of the first rectangle ($6 + 6 + 4 + 4 = 20$ centimeters). The second rectangle has the same perimeter, but has an area of 16 square centimeters. I know that a 2 by 8 rectangle has an area of 16 ($2 \times 8 = 16$) and a perimeter of 20 ($2 + 2 + 8 + 8 = 20$).
2. First rectangle: Possible answer: The area of the first rectangle is 24 square centimeters ($6 \times 4 = 24$) and the area of the second rectangle is 16 square centimeters ($2 \times 8 = 16$).

Week 35: Day 1 (page 183)
1. Quadrilateral has 1 pair of opposite sides parallel
2. Parallel means two lines that are the same distance apart and will never intersect.

Week 35: Day 2 (page 184)
1. Trapezoid; quadrilateral has 1 pair of opposite sides parallel; draw the shape

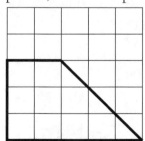

2. Rectangle: quadrilateral with 2 pairs of sides of equal length and 4 right angles; draw the shape

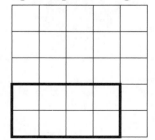

ANSWER KEY *(cont.)*

Week 35: Day 3 (page 185)

Rectangle: 2 pairs of parallel sides, 4 right angles, 2 long and 2 short sides; Trapezoid: 1 pair of parallel sides, 2 acute and 2 obtuse angles; Both: 4 sides (quadrilaterals), 4 angles

Week 35: Day 4 (page 186)

1. Possible strategies:

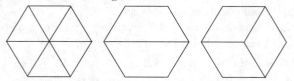

2. Possible answer: I think using 2 trapezoids to make a hexagon was easier because I saw it right away.

Week 35: Day 5 (page 187)

1. Square, rectangle, right triangle, right trapezoid
2. Square, rhombus, rectangle, parallelogram
3. No; Possible answer: The shape does not have a right angle and does not have opposite sides equal. The sides next to each other are equal.

Week 36: Day 1 (page 188)

1. square and hexagon divided into sixths
2. 6 equal parts; Possible answer: *Sixths* means six equal parts.

Week 36: Day 2 (page 189)

1. Divide square and hexagon into sixths; draw lines to make 6 equal parts
2. Divide circle and rectangle into eighths; draw lines to make 8 equal parts

Week 36: Day 3 (page 190)

Monique; $\frac{1}{3} > \frac{2}{8}$

Monique   Jessie

Week 36: Day 4 (page 191)

1. Plan B; Plan A: $3,000 × 6 = $18,000; Plan B: $5,000 × 4 = $20,000; Possible strategies: fraction models, multiplication and comparison, repeated addition
2. Possible answer: Drawing a fraction model was easier for me because it helped me see what the problem was asking me to do.

Week 36: Day 5 (page 192)

1. $\frac{1}{8}$; Possible drawings:

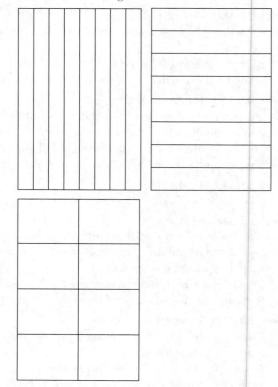

2. Yes; Possible answer: Since each rectangle is divided into equal parts, each part has the same area.

PRACTICE PAGE RUBRIC

Directions: Evaluate student work in each category by choosing one number in each row. Students have opportunities to score up to four points in each row and up to 16 points total.

	Advanced	Proficient	Developing	Beginning
Problem-solving strategies	Uses multiple efficient strategies Uses a detailed and appropriate visual model	Uses appropriate strategies Uses an appropriate visual model	Demonstrates some form of strategic approach Uses a visual model but is incomplete	No strategic approach is evident No visual model is attempted
Points	4	3	2	1
Mathematical knowledge	Provides correct solutions and multiple solutions when relevant Connects and applies the concept in complex ways	Provides correct solutions Demonstrates proficiency of concept	Shows some correct solutions Demonstrates some proficiency of concept	No solutions are correct Does not demonstrate proficiency of concept
Points	4	3	2	1
Explanation	Explains and justifies thinking thoroughly and clearly	Explains and justifies thinking	Explains thinking but difficult to follow	Offers no explanation of thinking
Points	4	3	2	1
Organization	Well-planned, well-organized, and complete	Shows a plan and is complete	Shows some planning and is mostly complete	Shows no planning and is mostly incomplete
Points	4	3	2	1

PRACTICE PAGE ITEM ANALYSIS

Directions: Record students' rubric scores (page 209) for the Day 5 practice page in the appropriate columns. Add the totals and record the sums in the Total Scores column. You can view: (1) which students are not understanding the mathematical concepts and problem-solving steps, and (2) how students progress after multiple encounters with the problem-solving process.

Student Name	Week 1	Week 2	Week 3	Week 4	Week 5	Week 6	Week 7	Week 8	Week 9	Total Scores
Average Class Score										

PRACTICE PAGE ITEM ANALYSIS *(cont.)*

Directions: Record students' rubric scores (page 209) for the Day 5 practice page in the appropriate columns. Add the totals and record the sums in the Total Scores column. You can view: (1) which students are not understanding the mathematical concepts and problem-solving steps, and (2) how students progress after multiple encounters with the problem-solving process.

Student Name	Week 10	Week 11	Week 12	Week 13	Week 14	Week 15	Week 16	Week 17	Week 18	Total Scores
Average Class Score										

PRACTICE PAGE ITEM ANALYSIS *(cont.)*

Directions: Record students' rubric scores (page 209) for the Day 5 practice page in the appropriate columns. Add the totals and record the sums in the Total Scores column. You can view: (1) which students are not understanding the mathematical concepts and problem-solving steps, and (2) how students progress after multiple encounters with the problem-solving process.

Student Name	Week 19	Week 20	Week 21	Week 22	Week 23	Week 24	Week 25	Week 26	Week 27	Total Scores
Average Class Score										

PRACTICE PAGE ITEM ANALYSIS *(cont.)*

Directions: Record students' rubric scores (page 209) for the Day 5 practice page in the appropriate columns. Add the totals and record the sums in the Total Scores column. You can view: (1) which students are not understanding the mathematical concepts and problem-solving steps, and (2) how students progress after multiple encounters with the problem-solving process.

Student Name	Week 28	Week 29	Week 30	Week 31	Week 32	Week 33	Week 34	Week 35	Week 36	Total Scores
Average Class Score										

STUDENT ITEM ANALYSIS

Directions: Record individual student's rubric scores (page 209) for each practice page in the appropriate columns. Add the totals and record the sums in the Total Scores column. You can view: (1) which concepts and problem-solving steps the student is not understanding and (2) how the student is progressing after multiple encounters with the problem-solving process.

Student Name:	Day 1	Day 2	Day 3	Day 4	Day 5	Total Scores
Week 1						
Week 2						
Week 3						
Week 4						
Week 5						
Week 6						
Week 7						
Week 8						
Week 9						
Week 10						
Week 11						
Week 12						
Week 13						
Week 14						
Week 15						
Week 16						
Week 17						
Week 18						
Week 19						
Week 20						
Week 21						
Week 22						
Week 23						
Week 24						
Week 25						
Week 26						
Week 27						
Week 28						
Week 29						
Week 30						
Week 31						
Week 32						
Week 33						
Week 34						
Week 35						
Week 36						

PROBLEM-SOLVING FRAMEWORK

Use the following problem-solving steps to help you:

1. understand the problem

2. make a plan

3. solve the problem

4. check your answer and explain your thinking

What Do You Know?

- read/reread the problem

- restate the problem in your own words

- visualize the problem

- find the important information in the problem

- understand what the question is asking

What Is Your Plan?

- draw a picture or model

- decide which strategy to use

- choose an operation ($+$, $-$, $\times$, $\div$)

- determine if there is one step or multiple steps

Solve the Problem!

- carry out your plan

- check your steps as you are solving the problem

- decide if your strategy is working or choose a new strategy

- find the solution to the problem

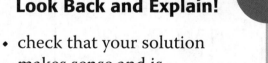

Look Back and Explain!

- check that your solution makes sense and is reasonable

- determine if there are other possible solutions

- use words to explain your solution

PROBLEM-SOLVING STRATEGIES

Draw a picture or diagram. 🍿 + 🍿 = 🍿🍿	**Make a table or list.** 	**Use a number sentence or formula.** $10 + 4 = 14$ $A = l \times w$
Make a model. 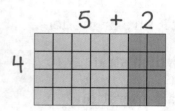	**Look for a pattern.**  **3, 6, 9, 12, 15,** __18__	**Act it out.** 
Solve a simpler problem. $7 + 6$ $7 + 3 + 3$ $(7 + 3) + 3$ $10 + 3 = 13$	**Work backward.** 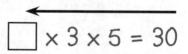$\square \times 3 \times 5 = 30$	**Use logical reasoning.** 
Guess and check. $2 \times \square + 5 = 13$ $2 \times 4 + 5 = 13$ $13 = 13$ Yes!	**Create a graph.** 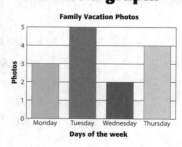	**Use concrete objects.** 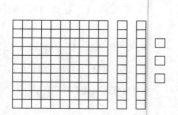 base-ten blocks

DIGITAL RESOURCES

Teacher Resources

Resource	Filename
Practice Page Rubric	rubric.pdf
Practice Page Item Analysis	itemanalysis.pdf itemanalysis.docx itemanalysis.xlsx
Student Item Analysis	studentitem.pdf studentitem.docx studentitem.xlsx

Student Resources

Resource	Filename
Problem-Solving Framework	framework.pdf
Problem-Solving Strategies	strategies.pdf

NOTES

NOTES

NOTES

NOTES

NOTES

NOTES

NOTES